DAN
ROB

Expert
ghost
hunter

DO YOU
BELIEVE
IN
GHOSTS?

Illustrated by

ELLEN
WALKER

CASE
FILE

PUFFIN

For my children,
Leo *and* ***Max****,*
who have promised to read this,
but only if I mention them
on the first page.

DO YOU BELIEVE IN GHOSTS?

PUFFIN BOOKS

UK | USA | Canada | Ireland | Australia
India | New Zealand | South Africa

Puffin Books is part of the Penguin Random House group of companies
whose addresses can be found at global.penguinrandomhouse.com.

www.penguin.co.uk   www.puffin.co.uk   www.ladybird.co.uk

First published 2025

004

Text design by Sarah Malley
Printed in Great Britain by Clays Ltd, Elcograf S.p.A.

The authorized representative in the EEA is Penguin Random House Ireland,
Morrison Chambers, 32 Nassau Street, Dublin D02 YH68

A CIP catalogue record for this book is available from the British Library

ISBN: 978-0-241-79824-9

All correspondence to:
Puffin Books
Penguin Random House Children's
One Embassy Gardens, 8 Viaduct Gardens, London SW11 7BW

Hello! Every time you see a little ghost next to a word – like this 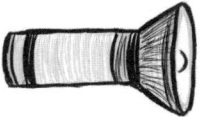 – you'll find some interesting extra information or a funny joke hidden somewhere else on that page. I call them **ghost-notes**.

So look out for them!

It's a bit like *Where's Wally?* – only with ghosts and information and funny stuff instead of Wallys.

Got that? Excellent. Because it's time to start our adventure. Someone once told me you should always begin a book with a question, so if you turn this page now you will find what I think is one of the **trickiest questions ever** in the whole of human history.

But if anyone can work out the answer, it's **YOU.**

....

This is how it works! Each ghost leads you to an extra fact or explanation! Like, for instance, did you know the first-ever ghost story that we have a record of is on an ancient stone tablet from **Mesopotamia** *(now called Iraq). It's 3,500 years old and it's in the British Museum!*

CHAPTER 1

DO GHOSTS EXIST?

DO YOU BELIEVE IN GHOSTS?

I've written it in MASSIVE CAPITAL LETTERS, but not because I'm SHOUTING VERY LOUDLY at you. That would be really rude, as we've only just met.

No, it's in such big writing because it's **REALLY IMPORTANT**.

It's a question we humans have been asking ourselves for thousands and thousands of years. And for me personally, it's something I have been thinking about my **entire life** – all the way back to when I was your age, doing exactly what you're doing right now.

I don't mean picking your nose and eating it or farting the tune to *Star Wars* under the bedcovers (though I'm pretty sure I was doing those things too, sometimes even both at once). No, I mean opening a book about ghosts, feeling fascinated, excited and – perhaps – just a little bit nervous. So, since you are at this *precise* moment, opening MY book about ghosts, I guess I should properly introduce myself.

What I call **snottyfartery**.

I'm **Danny** and I suppose you could call me a **ghost hunter**.

This is me.

Well, it's a cartoon version of me,[○] drawn by **Ellen**, who's illustrating this book.[○] You should probably meet a cartoon version of her too.

That's drawn by me. Maybe you can see why Ellen is in charge of the pictures.

I'll stick to the words and let her illustrate herself ...

....

[○] *My nose isn't actually **that** big.*

[○] *I have asked Ellen to reduce the size of my nose but she isn't replying to my emails!*

Phew, much better. Ellen and I met because she is a fan of my podcast. She enjoyed it so much that it inspired her to draw some

really cool cartoon versions of what happened in each episode, and she sent them to me, and I said 'Wow, would you like to come and illustrate my book?' So don't **EVER** let anybody tell you it's a bad idea to send cool stuff to people you like. You never know what might come of it!

My podcast is about ghosts and in each episode I investigate things that might be paranormal. '*Para*' is ancient Greek for 'beyond', so '**paranormal**' means literally anything 'beyond the normal', which is definitely a good way of describing what I do. Basically, I spend a lot of my time talking to people who think they might have seen a ghost and trying to help them solve the mystery of what happened.

The thing is, often when we hear the word

GHOST!!!!!'

our first thought is

SCAAAAAAAAAARY!!!!!

But actually, I think a much better word is

SPOOOOOOOKY

'Spooky' means getting that excited little tingle down your spine when you hear about something mysterious, unknown or intriguing. And being excited can't be a bad thing, right? It's the feeling I got when I first opened a book about ghosts as a kid all those years ago; the feeling I still get today when people tell me their ghost stories. It's the thrill of being able to try and solve some pretty cool mysteries.

*This time I **was** shouting loudly.*

'Scary', on the other hand, is a word that makes me think of being uncomfortable and wanting to run away – and why on earth would I write a book that makes you feel like that? I wouldn't have many readers if everyone who picked up my book sprinted out of the bookshop screaming

'NO WAAAAAAY AM I READING THIIIS BOOOOOOOOOK!!!!'

So, here is my solemn pinkie promise. This book is going to be full of spooky things – exciting, strange ghost stories full of seemingly impossible, astonishing happenings that we'll investigate together. **But you *won't feel scared*.** And if you do at any point feel even a little bit nervous, remember that is perfectly normal. Many adults feel that way about ghosts too. I think it's because human beings don't fully understand what ghosts are, and new things often make us tingly in our tummies – like starting at a different school, moving house or finding out you've been selected by the government as one of the first people to live on Mars.

But ... what if we *can* explain ghosts???? Wouldn't that be a pretty earth-shattering, universe-changing, eye-opening, mind-bending, amazing thing?

How you try to explain them depends on whether you are a **BELIEVER** or a **SCEPTIC**.

'Believers' think that ghosts are either the spirits of dead people coming back to haunt the living or some kind of mysterious supernatural energy we don't fully

---

*OK, this happens **slightly** less often than the other two ...*

Yes!

understand yet. 'Sceptics', on the other hand, think all these experiences can be explained by science, and that what people are seeing or hearing is not a ghost, but something completely normal in the natural world – like a creepy-looking shadow, an eerie creaking floorboard or something within our own imaginations. They don't think ghosts exist at all, but that the human mind just gets a bit too carried away sometimes.

So, what I want you to do for me right now is find a bit of paper and a pen or pencil, and write down which of these you think you are:

#TeamBeliever
or
#TeamSceptic

It's tricky, right? I'd say I'm a sceptic who really wants to believe. Ellen says she is a believer who thinks maybe she should be a little more sceptic.

Once you've done it, fold that bit of paper up and use it as your bookmark, and when we get to the end of the book, you can decide if what you wrote down is still how you feel. Or is it possible that some of the stories we're going to hear might change your mind...?

All right, now we've chosen sides and done any last-minute bogey-picking or farting, it's time to start our investigation. Our ghost-hunting team is me, Ellen and...

YOU.

Because this isn't like all those other books where the adventure happens to somebody else and you have to sit there patiently reading and waiting to find out what happens. You're going to be right there with us as we go on this paranormal mission together. We picked you to join our **ghost-investigating squad** because you are brilliant and clever and brave! (But also because we couldn't afford to pay for someone more famous, like a YouTuber, footballer or pop star.)

As you're going to be a really important team member, we've taken the liberty of drawing a cartoon

---

Your parents have agreed you will work for free as long as we feed you on every investigation. I hope you like biscuits?

version of you.  But because we have absolutely no idea what you look like, Ellen has drawn you with a ghostly bedsheet over your head.

That really suits you. You should DEFINITELY wear it to the next school disco and for your next class photograph. There's absolutely NO DANGER of your teacher **COMPLETELY FREAKING OUT AND *RUNNING AWAY SCREAMING***, trust me.

....

*When I say 'we', I mean Ellen. You really don't want to see the picture **I drew** of you! It made you look like a giant bogey.*

WHY DO PEOPLE THINK GHOSTS WEAR SHEETS?

Before coffins became commonplace, dead bodies were often buried wrapped in sheets called 'shrouds', and people imagined that, if the dead came back to life, that's what they'd be wearing.

In medieval times, some **cunning thieves** would even wear white sheets and pretend to be ghosts in order to scare people into handing over their money. Sometimes the victims got confused and thought the robbers really were ghosts, so the idea that ghosts wore sheets kind of stuck.

By Victorian times, it was common to see **theatre actors** on stage playing ghosts wearing sheets, and then, when TV and films came along, the tradition continued, which meant that more and more people all across the world started to see images of ghosts looking like this. These days, the majority of people in the UK aren't buried in a shroud, but we still think ghosts wear them!

*It's a great example of how things that are completely made up can come to be accepted as **utterly true** – which is something we should probably bear in mind as we start our investigation . . .*

So are you ready to dive into the strangest, most baffling and downright **weird** real-life ghost stories the world has ever seen? Some of them are famous, some are ones nobody has heard before.

This is the book I wish I could have read as a kid. Together, we're going to visit haunted houses, haunted schools, haunted workplaces and haunted battlefields. We'll meet people who think they've seen ghosts of queens, Romans, Victorians, fighter pilots, former owners of their houses and even a **famous rapper**. We'll hear about things flying across rooms as though thrown by an invisible hand, phantom footsteps walking down empty corridors and even a whole crowd of ghosts who walk through a wall.

With every case, we'll explore it from both points of view:

#TeamBeliever
and
#TeamSceptic

And each time, you can make up your mind about what YOU think really happened. It's going to be an amazing, baffling, mystical, magical quest. And at the end of it, I'll tell you all about one of the **spookiest** nights I have had in my life – an experience that really made me question what to believe. But before that, we'll learn all the special skills we need as ghost hunters to try and make sense of these spook-tacular paranormal mysteries, and hopefully, by understanding them, it means we can understand ourselves and our world a little bit better.

Does that sound like a plan?

....

*How's **that** for a cliffhanger?*

Feel free to answer out loud when I ask you questions. I can't hear you, but it will make people smile if you are sitting reading this book in public.

Excellent! Because we're going to start with one of the most famous ghost stories in British history, one that has had people arguing over what really happened for nearly half a century. It's a type of haunting that's weirder and freakier than almost any other, and you're really going to find it hard to explain what happens next . . .

It's time to meet a **poltergeist**.

*'What **is** a poltergeist?' I hear you say. Well, turn the page to find out . . .*

CHAPTER 2

THE MYSTERY OF 284 GREEN STREET

In which we discover an extraordinary ordinary house, meet a girl who may have superpowers and avoid a ghost who throws LEGO bricks.

D on't trip over your ghostly bedsheet, because we are walking down a street in Enfield, a quiet suburb of North London, heading for that house. Yep, that one over there. The completely normal-looking family home.

It's important to remember that not all haunted houses are creepy, medieval castles or historic stately homes. Some look very **ordinary**. Boring, even. But what happened inside this particular house back in the 1970s is definitely NOT ordinary, normal or boring.

The address is 284 Green Street and, since we are now cartoon versions of ourselves and therefore don't have to obey all the boring rules of physics that real humans do, we are going to teleport through time and space directly into the living room of this house, on the night of **4th September 1977**. Because that's when a LOT of people witnessed what they believed was poltergeist activity.

WHAT IS A POLTERGEIST?

'Poltergeist' is a German word that means 'noisy spirit'. It's how we describe ghosts that seem to have a **physical impact** on our world. This means you can actually hear them because they make scratching, tapping or LOUD BANGING noises, or they appear to make objects move – chairs sliding across rooms, plates flying off tables or, in one case I investigated, an electric toothbrush that kept turning itself on.

Perhaps it was the ghost of a dentist.

Some people who study poltergeist hauntings think that they happen in stages, with each type of spooky activity leading on to something even more extreme – like moving up a level in a computer game. Some parapsychologists  think it's because the poltergeist is trying stuff out, like a **naughty toddler** testing what its parents will put up with. Different experts have different ideas on the exact order of events, but most agree it's something like this:

THE POLTERGEIST SCALE

STAGE 1: *Strange, unexplained noises*

This could be scratching sounds or loud bangs. In a famous poltergeist case in Battersea, South London, in the 1950s, the bangs were so loud they woke the whole street up!

That's a fancy word for people who work at universities and study paranormal activity. How cool a job is that?

19

STAGE 2: Moving objects

This can be anything from tiny marbles to huge bits of furniture. In one case, it was believed a poltergeist had stacked a pile of chairs; in another, it allegedly made a bed lift into the air in front of three people!

STAGE 3: Apports and disapports

These are old-fashioned words meaning 'objects appearing' and 'objects disappearing'. Sometimes it's a personal thing like car keys, an item of clothing or a framed photo that disappears and then turns up somewhere else you know you didn't leave it. But other times it could be an object you have never seen before appearing in your house. One witness found tiny Buddha statues in the middle of his living room – he had absolutely no idea how they got there!

....

What's a poltergeist's favourite song? I Like To Move It, Move It!! (What do you mean that's a terrible dad joke? Look, you don't have to read these ghost-notes if you don't want to!)

STAGE 4: *Communication*

By this point in the haunting, it feels like whatever is in the house is trying to make contact! Perhaps it's through tapping sounds on a wall or table that seem to respond to questions, or, in the Battersea Poltergeist case, there were messages actually written in paint on the wall!

STAGE 5: *Destruction*

Sometimes things actually get broken! Whole rooms have been trashed in some cases, and there have also been hauntings where people believe the poltergeist started a fire!

STAGE 6: *Climax*

This means things reach an end. Sometimes this is because the people living in the house try to do something to get rid of the poltergeist, like calling a priest to perform an exorcism (a religious ritual to scare ghosts off), or sometimes the activity just stops by itself. No one really knows why this happens. Maybe, just like toddlers, poltergeists eventually get tired or bored of causing trouble!

Of all the poltergeist cases ever reported, the **Enfield Poltergeist** is the biggest and best known of all. It's the Real Madrid 👻 of polts, the GOAT of ghosts. People have written books about it, made documentaries, Hollywood films and even a West End stage show. All of these were aimed at grown-ups, which is a shame, because the main character in this story is an 11-year-old child.

Her name is **Janet Hodgson**, and she lives at 284 Green Street with her mum, Peggy, her older sister, Margaret, and her two younger brothers, Johnny and Billy. On this fateful night, as you, me and Ellen hide behind the sofa in a shadowy corner of Janet's living room, Janet is being carried through the open front door, fast asleep, in the arms of her neighbour, Mr Nottingham, a big burly builder.

....

👻 *Feel free to replace this with Barcelona, Bayern Munich, Paris Saint-Germain, or whichever team is doing best at football when you read this.*

Janet and her family have been staying with Mr Nottingham and his wife because of what's been happening in their house. It all started on 30th August 1977. The Hodgsons had heard strange knocks and bangs on the walls that they couldn't explain, and then, later that evening, Janet saw her brother Billy's bed 'going funny', as she described it – seemingly moving by itself. Which is weird, right? Weirder still, though – the next night, Janet's mum, Peggy, heard strange noises coming from the back bedroom, and when she went in to see what was going on, the noises seemed to be coming from a chest of drawers. Janet and Peggy both saw the chest of drawers move across the floor, and when Peggy tried to push it back, it wouldn't budge – it was as if an **invisible force** was stopping her!

Which is when Peggy decided to call the police.

Now, that might sound silly – dialling 999 to deal with a ghost – but think about it, what would you do, if you were frightened by something strange and didn't know how to make it stop?

So, at 1 a.m. on the morning of 1st September, the police came to check the house out. They couldn't find anything, but, just when they were about to leave, saying, 'sorry, there's nothing we can do', one of the officers, **PC Caroline Heeps**, saw a kitchen chair begin to wobble and slide about a metre across the floor, as if someone had pulled it!

So that is when Janet's mum got really frightened and took the kids to hide next door. The neighbours, Mr and Mrs Nottingham, didn't really know what to do either, but they suggested calling the *Daily Mirror* newspaper to see if they would come and investigate. Which is why, a few nights later, we have a journalist and a photographer standing here next to us in the living room. The photographer's name is Graham and he's holding his camera, looking a bit bored. You can probably hear him muttering to the journalist that it was a waste of time coming, because ghosts obviously don't exist – but then, just as he says that, something truly flipping extraordinary happens.

The exact moment that Janet is carried in by Mr Nottingham, **THINGS MOVE!**

Objects start flying around the room!

Look at them now – children's toys, marbles, an ashtray, lots of bits of junk you might expect to find in a 1970s family home, all swirling and hurtling around the dark living room like a mini hurricane!

And then –

'OW!!!!!' cries Graham the photographer. *'I JUST* **GOT HIT IN THE FACE** *BY A LEGO BRICK!!!!'*

Holy moly! Look at Graham's face.

There is indeed a lump above his eyebrow where he claims he's just been smacked by a potentially paranormally propelled bit of knobbly Danish plastic. And if you have ever accidentally

---

👻 *Lots of people smoked in their houses back then!*

stepped on a LEGO® brick, you will know just how painful those sharp edges can be. Imagine having one lobbed in your face at high speed by a ghost!

On the plus side, Graham now doesn't think it was a waste of time coming here, so he tells us to shove out the way to give him a better view and starts taking lots of photographs – *CLICK, CLICK CLICKING* away with his camera as fast as he can ...

GRAHAM MORRIS – WITNESS TO A POLTERGEIST?

Graham, the Daily Mirror photographer, is an entirely real person. His full name is **Graham Morris** and I met him to interview him for my podcast. A lot of what I know about the Enfield Poltergeist case comes from him.

What Graham experienced on 4th September 1977 changed his life, and he spent most of the next 18 months at the Hodgson family's house, trying to record what was going on and make sense of it. He felt like he witnessed lots of other weird, unexplainable things and the photographs he took are one of the best records we have of this case.

To this day, Graham is convinced there really was something strange happening at 284 Green Street, but he doesn't believe in ghosts! He thinks that paranormal activity will one day be explained by scientists, just like we now understand many things like electricity, space travel and computers, which would have seemed like magic to people hundreds of years ago.

Do Graham's experiences prove that poltergeists exist, or could he have been confused by what he saw? Can we always trust our own eyes? What do you think?

A few days after this night, Graham's photos from the house will be in the newspaper, and pretty soon Janet Hodgson will be one of the most famous people in the country, interviewed on BBC Radio 4 and then on TV too. Suddenly people around the world will be talking about this 11-year-old girl from Enfield, and how she seems to have a **ghost** in her home who throws stuff around.

So, does she?

Is there **really** a poltergeist in this North London house?

Or could there be another explanation entirely? I think it's time for you, me and Ellen to find somewhere to sit and work out our theories on what on earth is going on in this extraordinary ordinary house!

Are you ready to try and crack this case?

CHAPTER 3

FRIED EGGS AND FREAKY THEORIES

In which we contemplate spoon bending in a greasy-spoon cafe.

Right, I've found us a table in the greasy-spoon cafe near Janet's house. I ordered you a fried-egg sandwich (because they didn't have any fancy avocado on toast, granola and yoghurt, or chocolate croissants – this is the gloomy 1970s, after all!). Just try not to dribble any runny yellow egg yolk on that nice white bedsheet.

Outside the cafe, the sun has risen. It's the morning after the **SPOOK-TASTIC** night before. It's just as well our table is in a quiet corner where no one can overhear us, because we have some pretty mind-blowing stuff to discuss.

Let's start with flying LEGO bricks, shall we? How do we explain what Graham thinks happened to him?

Let's scribble some theories down on this napkin!

#TeamBeliever
theory –

It's NOT a ghost!

'WHAT????' I hear you say. 'Shouldn't that be a **#TeamSceptic** theory?'

Well, no, because this theory may not feature ghosts, but it does involve something that is very much paranormal – *psychokinesis*.

'**Psychokinesis**' is the idea that people can move objects with just the power of their minds. You might have seen it in movies and books – it's what Matilda does in the Roald Dahl story, and how Darth Vader and Luke Skywalker can make lightsabres fly towards their hands. Or think of Eleven in *Stranger Things* or

Jean Grey in Marvel's *X-Men*, who can concentrate on objects and get them to fly through the air. But surely it can't happen in real life, can it?

Well, there are people who believe it may actually be possible, and some paranormal researchers think it could play a role in poltergeist cases, thanks to something called **RSPK**.

Now, we know RSPB is the Royal Society for the Protection of Birds and RSPCA is the Royal Society for the Prevention of Cruelty to Animals, but what does RSPK stand for? The Royal Society for Performing Kangaroos? Pretending to be Koalas? Parachuting Kittens? Peeling KitKats? No, it stands for **Recurrent Spontaneous PsychoKinesis.** And just in case that particular collection of rather long words makes your head hurt, let me explain.

'Recurrent' means it happens again and again. 'Spontaneous' means it happens without you being able to control it. And psychokinesis ... well, we know what that means now. So, basically, this is the idea that a tiny percentage of people in the world, people

---

Yes, they **are** *cheating by having the P and the K in the same word!*

potentially like Janet Hodgson, are not having poltergeist activity happen *to* them, they are *causing it* – through some kind of electrical impulses in their brains that have the power to MAKE STUFF ACTUALLY MOVE without them even realizing they are doing it.

OMG. That really is pretty brain-scrambling. But why would this happen?

William G. Roll was a famous parapsychologist who first came up with the idea of RSPK in the 1960s. He believed it occurred when people reached a state of intense emotional turbulence inside them that

HIC CONFERENCE

then burst out! He thought this emotional state could be caused by going through a big moment in life, such as starting puberty and moving into adolescence, and certainly, a lot of poltergeist cases do have a teenager involved. Janet was nearly a teenager when this stuff happened to her.

It makes me think about the film *Inside Out*, where Riley's emotions have a real impact on what she does in the real world. But imagine if your emotions were somehow so strong they made objects move!

Photographer Graham Morris believes something like this was happening in the Enfield case. He told me that he once helped Janet with a science homework project, which involved moving iron filings across a sheet of paper using a **magnet** to show how magnetism worked, and he said, 'that's like you, Janet.' He believed that in 284 Green Street, Janet acted like a magnet, with the activity reacting around her.

COULD PSYCHOKINESIS REALLY BE POSSIBLE?

One of the most famous examples of someone who claimed they could use psychokinesis is Uri Geller, a former soldier, model and stage magician who became a star in the 1970s and 80s for going on TV shows and seemingly moving objects with his mind.

He appeared to be able to stop clocks just by looking at them and to be able to accurately describe pictures that were hidden from him. But his party trick was to make spoons bend with the power of his mind. Uri was so popular that he became a huge celebrity, releasing books, a board game, appearing in ice-cream adverts, being BFFs with pop stars, and he was even on the first series of I'm A Celebrity, Get Me Out Of Here!

Loads of children all over the world wanted to be like him and drove their parents mad by stealing spoons from the cutlery drawer and trying to bend them just by staring at them.

But there are plenty of sceptics that will tell you the seemingly miraculous feats Uri was performing were all stage illusions learned from his time as a magician. Magicians use tricks such as **misdirection** (distracting people) and **sleight of hand** (concealing things) to make people think that the impossible has happened.

I **so** know you are going to give it a go now!

The allegation was that Uri was switching spoons for pre-bent ones or using spoons that had been weakened so they would bend easily. Why don't you watch some clips of him on YouTube and see if you think he is genuine or faking it?

Incredibly, in 2019, after the Brexit vote, when the UK voted to leave the European Union, Uri wrote to the then British Prime Minister, Theresa May, telling her he was going to use the power of his mind to stop her taking the UK out of the European Union. It clearly didn't work though as, on 31st January 2020, the UK did leave! But who would have thought that we'd see a situation where paranormal powers tried to influence politics! Do you think ghosts should be allowed to vote? What about if we had a ghost as prime minister? Do you think they'd be **dead good?**

Sorry, that was a **terrible** joke. I bet you can come up with a much better one. I've put my email address at the back of the book. When you've finished reading, will you send me your best ghost joke, please?

#TeamSceptic
theory –

Somebody threw
the LEGO!

Before you get too worried, thinking 'I'm nearly a teenager, will I start seeing objects fly around my bedroom?', it's worth saying that if you are **#TeamSceptic** you absolutely do not think that psychokinesis is possible. In fact, you'd point out that there are several scientific laws that prove it is absolutely impossible!

Sceptics do agree with believers on one thing, though. They think that the person at the heart of a poltergeist case could be the cause of it. Not for paranormal reasons, though, but because they are **FAKING** it.

But hang on a second, why would someone want to pretend they had a poltergeist? It sounds pretty scary, right? Something to be avoided at all costs. And, in Janet's case, what happened in her home caused huge disruption and upset to her family. But some sceptics think that Janet enjoyed the attention she received when she started to become famous, and that she enjoyed it so much that she kept tricking people into thinking there was a ghost in her house so she'd get even more attention.

Sceptics who think like this suggest that the reason poltergeists sometimes behave like a naughty child (remember the **Poltergeist Scale** on pages 19–21) is because it actually *is* a naughty child who is causing these disturbances!

Some of the sceptical investigators who have looked at the Enfield case wonder if, in the dark living room that September night, Graham was deceived into thinking the LEGO brick flew towards him, when actually it was ***thrown by Janet*** or another member of her family!

Graham strongly disagrees. He doesn't think it's possible that someone could have thrown it without him noticing, and he also doesn't think they could have thrown it hard enough to injure him in the way it did.

I don't know about you, but I am feeling pretty torn right now about the Enfield Poltergeist. It does seem like Janet and her family were really frightened by what was happening in their house. There are also lots of independent witnesses to the strange events, including the police officer, Caroline Heeps. Would an experienced police officer really have been tricked by an 11-year-old child?

What are your thoughts? **It's time to vote!** Tell me – where's your head at right now on this amazing, spooky case?

 # TEAMBELIEVER

TEAMSCEPTIC

Better tick it in pencil though, just in case you change your mind – because this case definitely ain't over yet. And it's possible that flying LEGO bricks may just be the beginning of what happens to Janet. I've asked Graham to keep a keen eye on her and let us know as soon as any new activity happens, because right now we have somewhere else we need to be!

So finish those fried eggs and let's leave the cafe, cross the busy London road, full of double-decker buses, and head to the local train station. We have a long, long journey ahead of us, so we'd better jump on this express train that has pulled up. Mind the gap and keep your bedsheet clear of those closing doors, because we have **another** case to investigate – and if you thought poltergeists were weird, wait till you get a load of this one ...

You are about to actually SEE a ghost.

CHAPTER 4

AFTER DARK AT

R.A.F. LOSSIEMOUTH

In which we sneak on to a haunted air force base to meet a ghost and do our best not to get eaten as we travel back to prehistoric Britain.

We're flying faster than the speed of sound, because we've ditched the train and are now strapped into a supersonic, state-of-the-art Tornado GR4 fighter jet, zooming over the northern coast of Scotland. The North Sea glistens darkly below us as we reduce our speed, preparing for a night-time landing at RAF Lossiemouth air force base, the twinkling lights of the runway looming closer as we start our descent.

It's not a bad way to make an entrance for a paranormal investigation; there can't be many ghost hunters that break the speed of sound to crack a case! But our next haunting is lurking down there in the hangars full of military aircraft, and you might be excited to hear that this one involves an apparition! **'Apparition'** is the word parapsychologists use to describe ghosts that *actually appear* in front of you.

Sometimes people report them as being transparent – which means you can see through them. Sometimes they are described as a black shadow or grey figure. Occasionally people say they look as solid as you or me.

But whatever they look like, what we are talking about here is a **vision** of someone or something that, in theory, shouldn't be possible. Mostly that's because the vision is of someone who is dead but is now seemingly walking down the corridors of where they used to live. But in some extremely odd circumstances, there have been sightings of apparitions of **living people** who can't possibly be there, because they are actually in an entirely different place somewhere on the other side of the world at the very same time!

What do you mean I look more solid than you? Cheeky! OK, maybe I do need to lose a bit of weight, but all these ghost-hunting adventures make me **hungry** *... Though on the plus side, running away from ghosts is good exercise!*

FAMOUS APPARITIONS

ANNE BOLEYN

Anne Boleyn was King Henry VIII's second wife (and one of the unlucky ones to be beheaded by him!). She was executed at the Tower of London in 1536 and, ever since, there have been reports of people claiming to see her ghost, often without a head (gruesome, I know!).

The really interesting thing about Anne's ghost, though, is that she's not seen in just one place. As well as at the Tower of London, there have been sightings of her at Blickling Hall, near Norwich, where she was born, and Hever Castle in Kent, where she grew up.

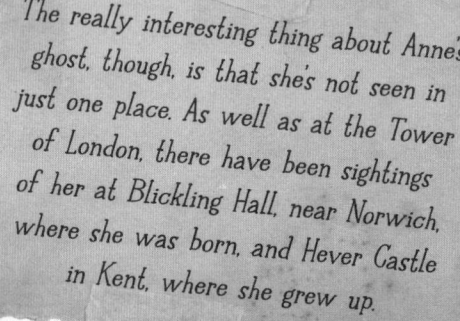

Is her ghost travelling between them? Perhaps on a phantom bike? Or has she become more than one ghost? Why don't you visit some of these places and see if you can spot her?

THE MAN IN GREY

Lots of theatres have ghost stories, but Theatre Royal Drury Lane in London's West End is said to be the most haunted theatre in the world. Its best-known ghost is the 'Man in Grey'. He's believed to be a nobleman dressed in a long grey coat and tricorn hat, with a sword. It's said that if an actor sees him, it brings good luck to their play.

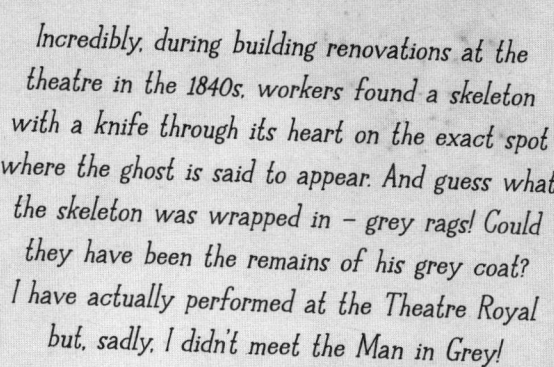

Incredibly, during building renovations at the theatre in the 1840s, workers found a skeleton with a knife through its heart on the exact spot where the ghost is said to appear. And guess what the skeleton was wrapped in – grey rags! Could they have been the remains of his grey coat? I have actually performed at the Theatre Royal but, sadly, I didn't meet the Man in Grey!

THE BROWN LADY
OF RAYNHAM HALL

Raynham Hall is a posh house in the Norfolk countryside and home to one of Britain's most famous ghosts. The Brown Lady is said to be the spirit of Dorothy Walpole, who died there in 1726. She was the sister of Robert Walpole, the first prime minister of Britain.

Dorothy was married to a rich man called Charles Townshend, who was also known as 'Turnip Townshend' because of his interest in farming turnips! He owned Raynham Hall and he had a very bad temper. The story goes that when he discovered Dorothy had fallen in love with another man, he cruelly locked her in her room and didn't let her out until she had died of smallpox!

People believe Dorothy's sad ghost is still trapped at the hall, walking the corridors in a brown dress. But the reason the Brown Lady became so famous is that some photographers from Country Life magazine were working at the hall in 1936 and took a photograph of the main staircase that they believed showed the Brown Lady in it! It caused a sensation around the world.

Maybe he shouldn't have spent so much time with **turnips** and done something more fun instead!

Here it is. What do you think? Does it show an apparition? Or is it a trick of the light?

Poltergeists might grab the news headlines, but I've always been intrigued by apparitions – what could be more definite evidence of ghosts, you might feel, than actually seeing one appear in front of you? I've always thought I'd like to see a ghost, but it also gives me that **tingly tummy** feeling. Do you know what I mean?

If the Enfield Poltergeist was world famous, then this next case we are going to investigate is the opposite. Absolutely no one else has heard about it before me and you. That's because I only found out about it when the witness who experienced it, a man called **Matt**, emailed to ask for my help in trying to make sense of what he saw. But other than that, he has kept this story to himself for the last 20 years!

You might think if you'd seen a ghost you'd want to tell the whole world about it, but I think people keep these experiences private for all sorts of reasons.

Sometimes they're worried about how they will be judged. Will people laugh if they say they saw a ghost, or even wonder if they have gone mad? But Matt has the added concern that his experiences took place on a **top-secret military base!** So please promise to keep everything he says to yourself, and whatever you do, don't let me do anything silly like write it all down in a bestselling book ...

Oh, and look over there – here Matt is now, dressed in his work overalls, crossing the tarmac of the runway as we climb out of the plane. Oh, and did I mention that we weren't just breaking the sound barrier up there in that Tornado GR4, we were also travelling through time again.

Because we've landed in the year 2004.

👻 **Hopefully** *bestselling, if you persuade enough of your friends to read it. No pressure.*

Tony Blair is prime minister, British military forces are fighting in Iraq and Afghanistan, and Matt is a 20-year-old aircraft engineer stationed here at Lossiemouth, in charge of keeping these expensive fighter jets in good working order for the fast-jet training squadron. Which is why he's walking towards that Land Rover, where his friend Simon is waiting, ready to drive them to the start of their night shift in Hangar K17.

They don't notice us duck into the back of their vehicle and stow away. We are spies, remember, here to observe, and we are timing our visit perfectly. Matt and Simon don't realize it yet, but tonight they are going to witness some **very strange happenings** that will make them utterly convinced they have seen a ghost, and we are going to experience it all with them! Are you feeling brave enough?

K17 is one of two large old hangars on the very edge of the airbase, originally built back in the 1940s when this was a Second World War base, sending planes off on bombing missions against Nazi Germany. Remember that detail, because it could be important later . . .

There's not much electrical lighting as we head towards this far-flung bit of the base. The star-filled sky feels huge above us and the cold Scottish night sends a shiver down my spine. What about you? Wishing you'd worn a warmer jumper under that bedsheet? These are all things we have to keep an eye on as we begin our investigation, because darkness and cold can confuse our senses and make us imagine things. And I am definitely starting to feel spooked out as the Land Rover stops next to the yawning, wide-open doors of Hangar K17. It feels like we are a long way from the light and warmth of the rest of the base. It's just Matt, Simon, us and a bunch of fighter planes sitting silently, waiting to be serviced, in the **pitch-black, chilling dark** . . .

WHY DO WE GET **SCARED**
OF THE DARK?

I know a secret about you. Something you'd never tell your friends. Something you wouldn't even admit to your family. That evening, a while ago, when you were asked to quickly pop to your bedroom and grab your socks for the wash, the reason you protested and refused to do it wasn't because you couldn't be bothered. **It was because you were scared to go into that dark room by yourself.**

How do I know? Because I've felt that same way too – and not just as a kid. There are plenty of grown-ups, people the same age as your parents (or even older!), who don't dare go into a dark room without turning the light on first. Some adults even insist on sleeping with a light on.

But why? It doesn't make any sense, does it? If a room is nice and cosy in the light, it doesn't suddenly become scary or dangerous in the dark. So what is it about our human brain that makes us start to imagine monsters lurking in those unlit, shadowy corners of a room?

To discover the answer, we need to do a quick detour from RAF Lossiemouth, all the way back to prehistoric times, when we were cavepeople huddling around one of those blazing hot things we'd just discovered how to light. A 'fire', I believe you call them. Apparently, they're getting very trendy.

Our neighbours in the next cave have invited us round to see theirs and here I am, happily grilling woolly-mammoth burgers  for dinner.

Major news – ghosts may exist, but bedroom monsters definitely don't. The scariest things you are likely to encounter in your bedroom are your **smelly socks**.

Very important to remove the wool before eating, or they can be quite **tickly** as you munch.

But outside the cave, away from the comforting glow of the flames, it is dark. And I mean **really dark**. We're going to have to wait a full two million years before electricity is invented. And we know that somewhere out in that pitch-black darkness, there really is a monster. Not a made-up one like we imagined in our modern bedroom, but a real and dangerous beast with long, sharp fangs who wants to steal our burgers and then eat us too. In fact, it is one of the most fearsome predators to stalk the Earth – a sabre-toothed tiger!!!

As modern humans, we are lucky – being chased by a predator is something we never need to think about. You don't pop to the shops and wonder if you're going to get eaten by a fierce animal. Or jump on a bus and expect to get swallowed whole by a wild beast. But cavepeople had to consider this every single day – and it wasn't just sabre-toothed tigers they had to fear, there were cave lions, bears and wolves too!

And the really bad news is these fearsome predators can do something we can't – they can see in the dark. So we know if we step away from the fire's light, we are at a major disadvantage and very likely to end up as food!

The good news, however, is that we have something our sharp-toothed enemies don't – fire! It's the flickering light of these flames that is scaring them off, stopping them from coming any closer.

And so there we have it – the reason why we modern humans are scared of the dark. The light was where our ancestors felt safe, and the dark was where they were in actual, literal danger. And it's how we still feel today.

It's an example of what psychologists call 'evolutionary psychology' – ways of thinking that are preprogrammed into our brains even before we are born. We don't **learn** to be scared of the dark as we grow up, it's just there in our minds – one of those bits of coding in the brain's natural computer that Mother Nature has kindly provided to help keep us alive.

But, like any computer system, things can get out of date and, in the same way you really don't need a CD-ROM drive on your home computer because nobody uses CDs now that we have cloud storage and streaming services, humans really don't need to be scared of the dark any more, because there isn't anything waiting out there to eat us these days. 🙂

So, try and remember this the next time you're feeling nervous about stepping into a darkened room in your house. It's still the same space that feels nice and comforting in the light, and the only reason you're feeling worried is because your old-fashioned brain is waiting to update itself to the new operating system!

COME ON, BRAIN – CATCH UP!!!
THERE IS NO REASON TO BE
SCARED OF THE DARK!!!

But let's get back to 2004. Matt likes the night shift here at Lossiemouth. From midnight until 7 a.m., while everyone else on the base is sleeping, a tiny

---

🙂 *Unless you live in a lion cage at a zoo. But, if you do, I think you really need to have a word with your parents about finding somewhere more suitable to live.*

crew of engineers work hard to make sure the planes are refuelled and serviced, ready for the morning's flights. And because everyone else is asleep, it means you get the run of the whole base to yourself, with no one there to tell you off if perhaps you secretly sneak into the officers' Operations Room to steal their tea and biscuits. (Everyone in the Air Force knows the officers always have much better biscuits.)

Sometimes, when they are having a cheeky cuppa and a stolen chocolate digestive, Matt and Simon like to look at the **old photographs** framed on the Operations Room wall. There are pictures of pilots who served here with the squadron many years ago, and souvenirs of old battles and missions, lots of them from the Second World War, when the Air Force was the last line of defence stopping the German Army from invading.

Occasionally, as they stand in the dark corridor gazing at the faces of these heroes from the past, admiring their smart, old-fashioned uniforms and impressive moustaches, Matt and Simon hear doors gently open and shut in other parts of K17. Their hearts skip a beat, thinking it must be an officer working late, coming to tell them off for raiding the biscuit cupboard. **But no one ever comes**. Matt and Simon check the other rooms, but they are always empty with the lights off. Whoever opened and closed those doors, it wasn't someone working late ...

At other times, they hear equipment moving – the sound of machinery and the chain hoists that are used to move heavy things raising and lowering. *It must be just wind blowing through the hangar*, Matt tells himself. But what kind of a breeze can move a 30-kilogram chain or make the sound of engineering equipment being switched on?

Matt isn't thinking about these things tonight though, because there is work to be done. He and Simon climb out of the Land Rover and go to check a Tornado jet on the other side of the hangar. Meanwhile, you, me and Ellen slide out the back of the vehicle unseen and hide behind a pile of fuel cans – a good place to observe anything that is about to unfold . . .

And that's where we stay for the next few hours. I don't know about you, but by 3 a.m., I am really starting to regret this plan. I'm cold and tired and want to be at home in bed. Absolutely nothing is happening! No apparitions! Not even a tiny bit of poltergeist activity. Nothing!!!

But of course, it's always just when you are about to give up that things do finally kick off. And in that strange part of the night, between 3 a.m. and 4 a.m. (people sometimes call it '**the witching hour**', when supernatural forces are said to be most likely to appear), Matt suddenly realizes that Simon has wandered off somewhere, leaving him alone in the hangar. We feel a crackle of tension in the cold night air and Matt's whole body stiffens as he swings his torch towards the door leading to the dark night outside.

'W-w-what was that?' he mumbles to himself.

Quick! Let's silently creep from our hiding place as fast as we can. We stand right behind Matt, as the torch swings in his shaking hand, its beam moving like a clock pendulum, back and forth across the open door, and then – caught in the light, I think I see what he sees too.

Do you?

Oh my goodness ...

What do you make of that?

It is ...

Without a doubt ...

(Well maybe just a bit of doubt, it is very dark after all ...)

But I would say *almost certainly maybe probably totally completely categorically abso-blooming-lutely* that it looks an **enormous massive huge substantial whopping chunky-wunky ginormous** amount like ...

A GHOST.

Or was it?

I'll meet you in the next chapter to find out ...

CHAPTER 5

THE HAUNTING OF HANGAR K17

In which we encounter something spooky stalking suspiciously among the supersonic jets, and learn that you can't always believe your own eyes.

Try saying that fast.

What it looked like, illuminated in that torch beam, was a **person**, pacing back and forth, at the point where the light of the hangar met the dark of the Scottish night outside. When we question Matt about it later, he says:

'It startled me, as I thought why and how is someone pacing in the dark? It was only a split second, but I caught the spin of a heel turning, followed by what looked like someone walking briskly in the opposite direction, into the darkness. At first I thought it was a fellow engineer, but with Simon having disappeared, I soon realized I was the only person anywhere near Hangar K17!

'When I thought about it later, I could have sworn the figure was a man in **dress blues** – that's the smart uniform for RAF pilots. Us engineers wear olive-green overalls with high-vis sleeveless jackets, normally. And I believe to this day that the person I saw was –'

Hold on a second, please, Matt.

Listen – and I'm talking to you now, not Matt. This is

REALLY IMPORTANT.

Before you hear the next thing Matt is going to say, I have a word of warning. It is spooky. And **weird**. Really, really weird. But don't worry, we're all here together, back in the well-lit, warm crew room, and I've found a packet of quite posh chocolate biscuits in the officers' biscuit cupboard to help us steady our nerves. So it's OK. Think *spooky* but not *scary*. Weird but not

WAAAAAAArRGGGHHHH!!!!!!!!

We can deal with this together.

Go on, Matt.

'I believe the person I saw . . .' says Matt, pausing for dramatic effect, 'was without a head.'

Yikes.

'Not in a gruesome way,' Matt continues. 'It wasn't like it had been chopped off or anything like that; it was just as if his head had been rubbed out by an eraser on a drawing, so all you could see of him was from the neck down.'

Blimey. It's quite something isn't it? Matt thinks he saw the headless ghost of an old RAF pilot! And that's not everything he experienced, either! When he went back into the hangar to finish the servicing of the aircraft, working as quickly as possible – because, let's be honest, we all wanted to get out of there as quick as we could by then – Matt had a really strange, uncomfortable sensation. I'll let him explain.

'One of my final jobs was to check the wheel bays on the Tornado, which involves sticking my head into a large cavity in the aircraft at chest height.

I did warn you.

As I did this, I had a sudden feeling, as if someone was right behind my shoulder, standing, waiting for me to dip my head out of the bay.'

Now we know it definitely wasn't us – we'd gone back to hiding behind the fuel cans by then. And Simon had disappeared. So who was it, walking around that empty hangar, creeping Matt out?

'It was such an **overwhelming** feeling,' says Matt. 'It felt like someone was literally stood at my back, almost about to touch me! It brought a cold panic and I froze! It took all of my strength and courage to bring my head out of the bay and, when I did . . . absolutely no one was there! I was so unsettled, I grabbed my toolbox and ran without looking back, all the way to the crew room.'

Which is where we find ourselves now. And as poor Matt goes off to make himself a strong hot chocolate to steady his nerves, I think you, me and Ellen should regroup over here in this empty room where they normally train new pilots, to see if we can work out what in the name of flying thunder is actually going on in Hangar K17 . . .

OK, shut the door and listen up, cos there are a LOT of thoughts racing round my head. I'm going to get Ellen to scribble them down on this conveniently placed whiteboard.

#TeamSceptic theory –
It's all in the MIND

Some children's books will try and explain complicated things to you in very simple ways with lots of short words. Or worse, they won't even bother explaining them **at all** because they don't think you are grown up enough to understand. But that is really patronizing and insulting. You might be a child, but you're not stupid! In fact, I often think that children are the cleverest people in the world. It's the dumb adults who normally mess everything up. So, I'm now going to explain something to you that's a bit complicated, but because you are so clever, I know you'll understand it!

COGNITIVE BIAS

'Cognitive' means to do with the way we think and process information with our brains. 'Bias' is when someone believes one thing is better or more important than another. For instance, you can be biased about one football team over another. Or, in a less nice sense, sometimes people can show bias against other people. For example, they may not give them a job, simply because of how they look or what their religion is.

So 'cognitive bias' is when people think in certain ways, and are therefore more likely to believe certain things and not believe others. So, for instance, if you already think a building might be haunted, and then you see a spooky-looking shadow or hear a freaky-deaky noise, you are more likely to be biased towards believing that it could be a ghost. And if you are already certain that it's a ghost, you will be biased against any sceptical explanations.

And remember, before Matt's experience, he had heard all those odd noises late at night. He had started to convince himself that Hangar K17 might be haunted. And what about those old photos of long-dead pilots with old-fashioned uniforms on the Operations Room wall – the souvenirs from Second World War missions? Is it possible that Matt had stored those images in his head and then, when he saw a shadow outside the base, he imagined it could be the ghost of one of those pilots?

But, but, but – I hear you say – Matt is a **sensible guy**, he's a trained military engineer! He might be an adult, but he's not one of the really dumb ones. Why would he think a random shadow was a person walking around?

It's an extremely good question, and to answer it we need to think back to that caveperson campfire we were sitting around in the last chapter, staring out into the prehistoric darkness. Those sabre-toothed tigers, cave lions, bears and wolves weren't the only threat out there. There was also the ever-present possibility that other cavepeople from a rival tribe might turn up and attack you to steal your mammoth burgers, probably clubbing you over the head with a stone axe and killing you in the process.

In fact, because these other humans had weapons, they were probably even more dangerous than the animals, so our brains taught us to be really good at spotting **them** too. Humans are experts at instantly recognizing the shapes of bodies and recognizing faces, even in lowlight conditions, so that while we can't see well in the dark, we can do our absolute best to spot any potential human threats.

....

Well done. Top marks.

But we don't always get it right. Sometimes what we identify as a figure isn't that at all.

This is why that bookcase in the corner of your room, or the dressing gown on the back of your door, can sometimes look like a person – it's because it is better to be wrong than dead. Mistaking a shadow for a person isn't going to cause you any problems, but *not* spotting a person with a big stone-age club determined to bosh you on the head might be the last mistake you ever make.

So, yeah, we get things wrong all the time – jumping at shadows, imagining they're ghosts or monsters – and **spooking ourselves out** so much that we jump at even more shadows, or little noises, or tiny gusts of wind, until everything we feel, see or hear feels like evidence of a ghost.

Could that be what is happening to Matt?

Maybe ...

But what if I told you that Matt was not the only person to have a spookaloopy experience in Hangar K17?

What if I told you someone else had an experience there that was even **WEIRDER?**

Because who should we find when we walk back into the crew room at the end of the night shift? It's Matt's friend Simon. Remember he had disappeared and left Matt alone? Well, Simon wasn't off somewhere nice putting his feet up, relaxing. He was getting well and truly freaked out himself by his very own potential ghost!

I think we'd better interview him, don't you? (Prepare to be spooked!)

SIMON'S ENCOUNTER

Simon is talking really fast and hopping from one leg to another and swearing quite a bit – which is not like him at all, and of course not something I approve of  – but you might have noticed that swearing is what adults sometimes do when they get a big shock. Like when they drop something on their toe, or realize they've forgotten their keys, or find out the cost of that computer game you want for Christmas ... or when they think they might have seen a ghost.

....

I swear to you that I never swear.

Simon's face is as white as your bedsheet and he is breathing very heavily – big, deep, trembly breaths, as he tells Matt what he experienced.

'I was doing the last checks on the aircraft,' Simon says. 'Walking from the plane's tail to its nose. As I approached the centre of the aircraft, I saw a pair of legs and boots on the other side of the plane. They seemed to be walking the opposite way to me – going from the tail of the plane to the nose.

I assumed it was you, Matt, coming over to help me with the final checks, so I started chatting away, you know, like we normally do. As the legs moved along to where the plane's fuselage gets narrower though, I could see the boots and trousers more clearly, and then, as the legs reached the nose of the aircraft . . . They disappeared!

Apart from the bits where you spilt egg yolk. And the chocolate biscuit stains. Don't think I didn't notice!

They just faded away to nothing. One minute I was looking at them and then the next, they had gone.

I walked around the plane's nose and there was absolutely no one there!

I know what I was looking at was really there, I can remember it so clearly – the little details. And the more I thought about it, the more those details seemed ... odd. The boots were brown pilot boots, lined with fleece, which seemed a bit old-fashioned. And the trousers, which were tucked into the boots, were a greeny-blue woollen weave. As you know, these aren't the kind of clothes that pilots or crew wear now, they're the sort of thing they'd have worn a long time ago, like... back in the Second World War!

I was so freaked out that I just panicked and ran out the hangar!'

Blimey.

I know I already said blimey earlier. But this is the kind of case that makes you say blimey quite a lot. In fact, I'm going to have to go for another one.

BLIMEY.

Now we know why Simon left Matt alone, and we have not one but *two* incredibly strange and detailed accounts from two very sensible witnesses who are pretty sure they saw what looked like a ghost pilot ...

So how are we feeling about this case now? Do you think what is happening at RAF Lossiemouth is genuinely paranormal or something we can explain environmentally or psychologically?

Better tick that box!

 # TEAMBELIEVER ☐

TEAMSCEPTIC ☐

But use pencil again because, before your mind gets too made up, remember we've only discussed the #TEAMSCEPTIC theory.

It's time to hear a **#TeamBeliever** theory and it's one I think will truly blow your mind. To understand it, we're going to have to hit the road again. Because the best way I can think of to explain this theory is to take us to a dark, dank old cellar under the ancient streets of a very historic British city. In fact, it's what people sometimes claim is the *most haunted* city in the whole of the UK. It's full of incredible ghost stories (there's one on almost every street!) but this cellar I'm taking you to was the scene of the strangest and most convincing of them all. And I think it's a story that might just hold the key to helping explain what happened to Matt and Simon.

All I'm going to tell you is that it involves Romans.

A **lot** of them.

Intrigued?

Can you guess where we're going yet?

Turn that page to find out ...

CHAPTER 6

THE ROMANS

IN THE

CELLAR

In which we nearly get
stomped on by Roman soldiers
and learn about the
ancient, mysterious art of
recording things off the telly.

D on't tell Matt, but I borrowed one of his Tornado jets, and have just supersonically chauffeured us down the north-east coast of the UK, to the county of Yorkshire, and one of my all-time favourite places in Britain – **York**.

After a brief stop in a cafe for a sandwich,  we now find ourselves strolling along this ancient city's historic cobblestone streets, lined with houses that date back to Tudor times and even older.

I had cheese, you had jam, but don't worry, I won't tell your parents. Ellen had chocolate spread. I will be telling her off – once I've eaten the crusts she left behind.

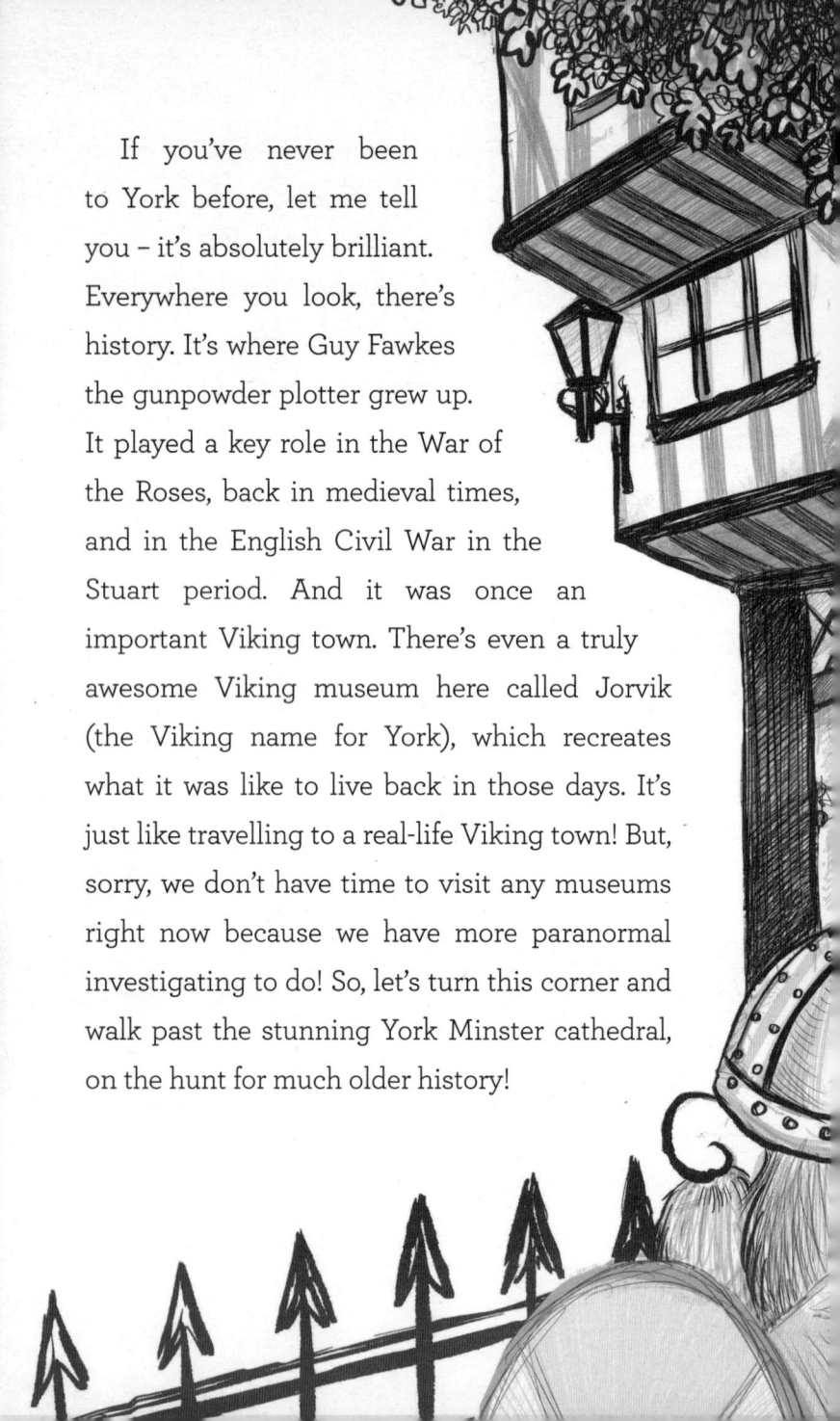

If you've never been to York before, let me tell you – it's absolutely brilliant. Everywhere you look, there's history. It's where Guy Fawkes the gunpowder plotter grew up. It played a key role in the War of the Roses, back in medieval times, and in the English Civil War in the Stuart period. And it was once an important Viking town. There's even a truly awesome Viking museum here called Jorvik (the Viking name for York), which recreates what it was like to live back in those days. It's just like travelling to a real-life Viking town! But, sorry, we don't have time to visit any museums right now because we have more paranormal investigating to do! So, let's turn this corner and walk past the stunning York Minster cathedral, on the hunt for much older history!

You see, the origins of York go all the way back to 71 CE,🗯 when the Romans founded a city here, which they called Eboracum. Remains of the ancient buildings that formed that city still lie buried under modern-day York. It's a bit like the **layers of a cake**, one on top of the other. And the bottom layer – the first bit of chocolatey sponge, if you want to think of it like that🗯 – is the nearly 2,000-year-old foundations of Eboracum's villas, bathhouses, military barracks and shops. So there's every chance that, as we munched our lunch in that cafe earlier, we were sitting directly above the ancient Roman supermarket where they used to buy pickled dormouse for their lunch.

Imagine if the stones of those old buildings could tell stories! What would they say to us about the way people used to live in this city? It would be fascinating, wouldn't it, getting all that ancient Roman gossip?

Well, what if I told you that maybe those stones **can** tell stories?

....

🗯 *That's exactly 1,954 years before I wrote this book. Not even your* **grandparents** *were alive then.*

🗯 *I definitely do. I love chocolatey sponge.*

How amazing would that be???

You'd better get ready for . . .

#TeamBeliever *theory* –

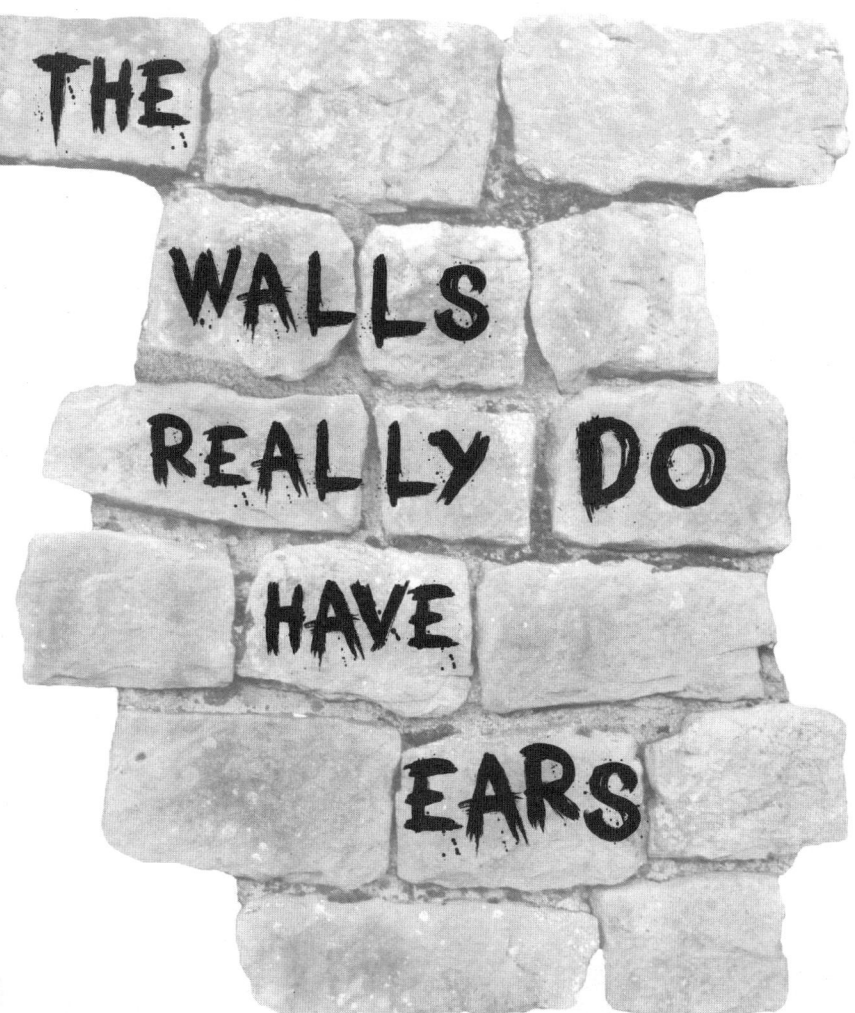

THE WALLS REALLY DO HAVE EARS

This might seem like an odd question, but have you ever heard of a VHS tape?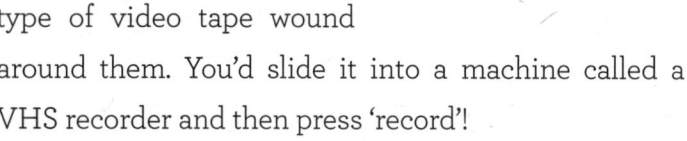

It's how we used to record things off the telly, back in the olden days of the 1980s and 90s, when people as truly ancient as me and your parents were growing up. Google it and you'll see what they looked like – a black plastic rectangular cassette, as chunky as a brick, with two plastic circular reels inside it that had a special type of video tape wound around them. You'd slide it into a machine called a VHS recorder and then press 'record'!

In the modern world, where we can use a phone or laptop to watch any video we want on YouTube, Netflix, Disney+ or Amazon, it probably seems to you like a ridiculously old-fashioned technology, having to store all your recordings on great big lumps of plastic.

....

*It stands for Video Home System. Not particularly exciting, I know. If I'd had **my** way, it would have stood for Volcano Holiday Surfing or Vegan Horse Samurais.*

But when I was a kid this was an incredible invention, because before VHS tapes, the only way people could watch TV programmes was to catch them live at a certain time! Can you even imagine that? Having to sit down at exactly 5.30 p.m. or you'd miss your favourite programme? But suddenly, with VHS tapes, we had the power to record our favourite shows and watch them whenever we wanted – it was **REVOLUTIONARY!**

And the way they worked was that the tape itself was coated with iron oxide particles, which are magnetic. When you pressed 'record' on the VHS player, electrical signals were sent from the machine, through the **iron oxide particles** on the tape, converting them into magnetic patterns that recorded and stored the light and sound from the TV. Then, later on, when you pressed 'play', this light and sound reassembled itself into the right magnetic patterns to show the programme you recorded.

Sounds a bit complicated, right? (Though also pretty cool.) But why am I telling you this? **'VHS TAPES HAVE *NOTHING TO DO WITH GHOSTS*, DANNY!!!!'** I hear you shout.

Well, stop shouting right now,[👻] because they might have *everything to do with ghosts*.

Some buildings, and even the ground itself, can also contain iron oxide particles, just like those video tapes. And there are paranormal experts who believe that those particles might also be able to record stuff. Except in this case it's not 1980s TV programmes, but instead, actual historical events that happened in that place.

It's called **Stone Tape Theory**, and it's basically the idea that the stones of the building you are in, or the land you are standing on, behave like one giant VHS tape, and that when you think you're witnessing a haunting, you are actually seeing a 'recording' of something from long ago, playing back in the same exact spot where it happened, like a ghostly video.

This could be something as simple and ordinary as a Victorian person who used to own your house walking up and down the stairs. But often the theory is linked to places where something really dramatic and shocking happened – such as a battle. One of the

---

👻 *Please. It was hurting my ears.*

most famous battlefields in Britain is Culloden, near Inverness in Scotland. It's where the Scottish leader Bonnie Prince Charlie, who tried to claim the British crown, was defeated by the English in 1746, when his army of 'Jacobite' Scottish rebels were brutally slaughtered there. Every year, on the anniversary of the battle, 16th April, people claim they can **hear the sounds** of the two armies fighting – swords clashing, horses whinnying and wounded soldiers crying out in pain – as if it was still playing back nearly three hundred years later.

*In all the popular stories, paintings and songs of the time, Bonnie Prince Charlie is made to look like a dashing Scottish prince wrapped in tartan, but he was actually born in **Italy** and grew up there until his twenties – it's another example of how you can't always trust what people tell you. If you want to be a ghost hunter (or a historian) you need to question everything and always check your facts!*

It's an interesting thought, isn't it? And, just like RSPK, which we explored in the Enfield case, Stone Tape Theory suggests ghosts aren't literally the spirits of the dead deciding to return to our world and spook us out for a bit of a laugh, but instead, are more like a kind of **highlights reel** of historical things that happened in a particular place – the echoes of our ancestors, which I personally happen to think sounds like an even cooler idea than VHS tapes. In fact, it's one of the coolest things I have ever heard, and I hear lots of cool stuff, trust me. It is also the whole reason we have come to York and why we are right now walking downstairs into this cellar – mind that bedsheet on those steps and don't bang your head!

Remember Uri Geller and the bending spoons? Did you give it a go?

Because something happened in this cellar that a lot of people believe proves that Stone Tape Theory is actually real. It's a potential haunting that is 100% totally weird. So, I guess now we're down here in the dark of the cellar, I'd better fill you in on exactly where we are. You are currently standing directly beneath the **Treasurer's House**, a historic building that dates back to Tudor times, and I'm going to ask you to take some really deep breaths and then hold your nose.

I mean it.

Seriously. I know some books say stuff they don't mean, but I want you to concentrate hard and breathe in, and breathe out, because we are going to travel through time again to visit this cellar in the year when this potential haunting happened. So, if you're ready, hold your nose – don't be tempted to pick it, and absolutely **no unauthorized farting**, please –

because we are jumping back to ...

---

*It's a well-known fact that farting while time travelling can send you to the wrong period entirely. I once met a man who had let a particularly **stinky** fart off while trying to travel to ancient Egypt and found himself in 1980s Birmingham instead. You can imagine how disappointed he was.*

1953!

Phew, we did it! And here we are now in the same cellar, just a few years after those Second World War pilots were flying their missions from RAF Lossiemouth. In 1953, Britain is still recovering from the war, rationing[🔔] is still in place, it's the year that Sir Edmund Hillary and Tenzing Norgay became the first people to climb Mount Everest, and Elizabeth II was officially crowned Queen of England. Life was pretty different back then, but this cellar looks pretty much the same, except there is someone else here with us now – look over there – can you see the young man in overalls?

He's only 18 and his name is **Harry Martindale**. One day, when he is older, Harry will become a police officer, but right now he's an apprentice heating engineer, helping to install a boiler as part of a new central heating system to keep the Treasurer's House warm. He's down here alone, and, as you can see, he's

---

[🔔] **Rationing** *was a system of rules stating how much food people were allowed to buy. They were brought in during the war to deal with food shortages. The war ended in 1945 but rationing stayed in place until 1954! Imagine having to go without enough of your favourite foods for that long!*

up a ladder, trying to knock a hole in the brick ceiling to run a heating pipe through. So we'll just park ourselves over here, shall we, in a shadowy corner on the other side of the room (one of the key rules of time travel is to watch but not get in the way).

We needn't worry too much, though. Harry, always a hard worker, is entirely focused on his job, until . . .

BUUH-DUUUHH!!!!!

Did you hear that? It sounded like a trumpet blast. Harry thinks it must be coming from upstairs, maybe from a radio? But then –

BUUUUUUH-DUUUUHHHH!!!!!

It's even louder this time! It has a military sound to it, like someone is summoning the troops, calling them to assemble!

BUUUUUUUH-DUUUU

Oh my goodness – that third one really made me jump! And Harry too, by the looks of it – he is really wobbling on that ladder now. The noise felt like it was coming from just the other side of the wall to where he's working. And then, immediately after the third blast, something very strange happens.

A helmet starts to appear, as if it was pushing itself through the wall! It's a Roman helmet, which seems to be attached to an actual Roman legionary's head! Oh crikey, yes, and there's his body too, in full armour, now visible as he seemingly walks through the solid brick wall!

Which is, of course, utterly impossible.

UHHHH!!!!!!!

'**OUCH!**' moans Harry. Oh no! We might be used to witnessing the impossible after our experiences with Janet's flying LEGO bricks and Matt and Simon's apparitions, but this is all new to Harry. He is so surprised by what he's just seen that he has fallen off his ladder! And now he's picking himself up and scuttling away to hide, as we all watch this bizarre scene unfold. Because it just gets stranger and stranger...

The first legionary is followed by another. And this one is riding a horse!

And then more soldiers emerge from the wall, walking two abreast, until there are twenty of them in total, marching through the cellar,

completely oblivious to Harry, who lies there terrified, wondering what in the name of Julius Caesar is happening in this cellar under York where, until a few moments ago, the most important thing to think about was whether he could successfully install a heating pipe.

But Harry, remember, will one day be a police officer. He's a sensible guy, and so he doesn't let his trembly-legged fear completely overtake his **powers of observation**. He studies the Romans in forensic detail and he notices some strange, confusing things.

Because we all know what Roman soldiers look like, right? We've seen them in history books and TV programmes and films. They wear red tunics under their distinctive armour and they carry those very recognizable rectangular, curved shields.

Except these Romans *don't* look like that. They are wearing green tunics and they have round shields.

But weirdest of all are the legionaries' legs.

Because one other thing we know about Romans is . . . that they had **feet**. And if you look closely, these ones don't! All of the Romans marching past poor startled Harry can only be seen from the knees up! It's as if their lower legs have entirely vanished – just like the head of Matt's pilot – but in this case, their missing bits are somehow hidden below the ground. And then, these 20 men and one horse all **disappear** through the opposite wall, just as strangely and suddenly as they appeared!

DID THE ROMANS INVENT HAUNTED HOUSES?

Did you know that the first-ever work of literature to feature a haunted house was written by a Roman? It's a play called **Mostellaria**, by the Roman playwright Plautus.

The Romans were very interested in ghost stories. Another famous Roman writer, **Pliny the Younger** (he had an uncle called Pliny the Elder!), wrote a story set in Athens in Greece, which features a philosopher named Athenodorus, who rents a house haunted by a ghost that **rattles chains** to scare him. Later in the story, Athenodorus discovers a body under the house, bound in chains. When he gives him a proper burial, the ghost goes away! It's been the inspiration for so many other ghost stories since and, even today, when people want to make ghostly sound effects, they often rattle chains!

So next time someone tries to tell you a story about a haunted house, why don't you tell them it was a Roman invention?

In the silence that follows the disappearance of the ghostly legionaries, the only sound in the cellar is Harry's panicked breathing, as he tries to recover from witnessing a platoon of 2,000-year-old soldiers walking past him.

What would **YOU** do if you'd just witnessed this?

Would you tell anyone?

How would you even begin to describe it?

Would you be worried that your friends or family might think you were lying or making it up? Or even that you were hallucinating?

Harry is asking himself all of these things. And later, when he does tell a few people, they do mostly think that he is lying or was imagining it. Because we all know Roman soldiers don't wear green or carry round shields and that they do have feet.

Until . . . years later, when excavations by archaeologists under the Treasurer's House reveal that it sits exactly on top of the site of one of the major Roman roads in York (or **Eboracum** as it was called back then) – the **Via Decumana**, a road that led right out of the military fort where legionaries would have been stationed. That road was our chocolatey sponge – the base layer under this Tudor cellar – and do you want to know how much lower than the floor of the cellar it would have been?

About the distance between your knee and your foot.

So if Harry really did see those Roman soldiers, perhaps their legs hadn't disappeared – they were simply **hidden** beneath the floor because the legionaries were walking on the original Roman road, underneath the cellar! Because, just possibly, they were a recording playing back, marching the same route they took in life, ignoring the modern floor level.

Brain-boggling, isn't it?

And what about those other odd details Harry spotted? Well, many more years after Harry's experiences, historians discovered that there was a legion of auxiliary soldiers stationed in York that had ... wait for it ... drumroll please ...

 ## Green tunics and round shields.

So did we really just witness Stone Tape Theory in action, like a Roman-era VHS tape rewinding across the cellar? And if we did, and it means that this particular theory could actually be possible, does that change how we feel about what Matt and Simon saw in Hangar K17? I'm thinking of those phantom legs dressed in old-fashioned pilot's gear, and the strange headless figure in RAF dress uniform. Could they have been witnessing something similar – just a little bit of history repeating itself?

Sceptics and scientists will be quick to tell us a whole host of good reasons why Stone Tape Theory can't be possible and why the atoms of **stones** cannot behave like VHS tapes. But believers will ask, 'How else do we explain these hauntings? Doesn't it feel just like a recording playing back?'

I think one of the nice things about paranormal investigation is that there is no right or wrong.

Hauntings aren't like a maths test or English grammar homework. However you try to explain them, it's just an opinion. Maybe, in many years' time, when you have grown up, and I am a tiny wizened old man with a long beard like Gandalf, extremely knobbly knees and a walking stick, somebody ingenious will have finally found a clever way to prove what ghosts definitely are. But until then, all we can do is go with our instincts and our gut feelings.

So, after all you have heard so far, from 284 Green Street in Enfield to RAF Lossiemouth in Scotland, and this historic cellar under the city of York, I am asking where your head is at.

 **#TeamBeliever**

#TeamSceptic

Has what you ticked here changed from the beginning of the book? Or are you rock solid in what you think? Either way, there is still plenty of time to switch sides because we have some incredible cases to come and, I don't know about you, but investigating all these mysterious, baffling, spookaloopy stories is making me think

one **BIG** thought...

It's all very well to *see* ghosts. That is certainly impressive. But if we really want to make sense of the paranormal, wouldn't it be a good idea to actually try and **speak** to a ghost? To ask it *why* it was haunting us? Who or what it really is? If you are feeling brave enough, I think you are now ready for a whole new stage in our supernatural adventure . . .

It's time to communicate with the spirits.

I know that sounds a bit **scary**. Don't worry. Remember my **spooky promise!** *I'm here at all times to protect you and, if things do go wrong, I have kept the Tornado jet for a quick getaway. Just don't tell Matt!*

CHAPTER 7

KNOCK KNOCK

WHO'S THERE?

In which we cross the Atlantic to summon the dead, discover a ghost who knows everything and meet a family of fantastic Foxes with a shocking supernatural secret.

Kate and Maggie Fox are sitting on the bed. '**Count to five**,' says their mum. But she's not talking to the girls. They are 11 and 14 years old. It wouldn't be very impressive if they counted to five. I mean, we can all do that, right?^[👻] No, she is talking to something else. Something invisible. Something that, just seconds later, answers:

THUD!

THUD!

THUD!

THUD!

THUD!

From where we are hiding, peeking out from behind the girls' wardrobe, it sounds like the noises are coming from the floor. Loud, heavy bangs. Exactly five of them.

👻 *You **can**, can't you?*

'Now count to fifteen!' says Mrs Fox.

There's just a moment's pause, then the banging starts again – you can count them with me:

THUD THUD THUD THUD THUD THUD – six –
THUD THUD THUD – nine –
THUD THUD THUD THUD – thirteen –
THUD THUD – fifteen.

Each one clear and distinct.

Mrs Fox looks both shocked and impressed. Kate and Maggie had told her about the strange noises they could hear in their bedroom, and how the sounds seemed to reply when they asked questions. Now she is witnessing it for herself, first-hand.

And so are we, having just transported ourselves directly into that bedroom. It's been quite a journey to get here. I'll tell you about it in a moment, but

right now we are observing something truly remarkable. Is this really a ghost who replies when you ask it questions?

Also standing here shocked and dumbfounded is Mrs Fox's neighbour, who'd heard the gossip about the odd banging and decided to pop over to see what all the fuss was about. She came expecting to laugh it off, but, well . . . she ain't laughing now. Whatever it is that's booming out from under the floorboards of the Fox family's farmhouse 🙂 is getting **everything** correct. Which makes it pretty unlikely that it's mice or raccoons or a stray cat making the noises. Even the most intelligent cats I have met can't count. 👻

Mrs Fox decides to try a **trickier** question. She asks the thing under the floorboards to tell them the neighbour's age. Surely this will have it stumped?

We wait for a tense moment. (I'm tempted to do a drum roll but worry that might confuse matters . . .)

....

🙂 *This is a family of* **humans** *with the surname Fox by the way, not a family of actual foxes. Sorry, but if you're after that kind of story I suggest you go and read a Roald Dahl book instead, because I can't help you!*

👻 *I am always ready to be proved wrong. If* **you** *know a cat who can count, I would love to meet them.*

And then, we hear *thirty-three* **THUDS** on the floor, one after another. The neighbour is stunned. Flabbergasted, in fact. Because she is indeed 33 years old. How could it possibly have known this?

We all look down at the floor. What is this strange being we are seemingly communicating with? And doesn't it realize that no adult ever wants to be reminded of their real age? You ask your parents right now if they'd like a ghost to tell everyone how old they are. See what they say. (In fact, if there are any ghosts reading this, I demand you tell everyone I am still 21 and a half.)

But we're getting sidetracked . . . the important thing to remember is that everyone in this bedroom is now feeling pretty **FREAKED OUT** because we appear to have just had an intelligent conversation with an invisible being. And no one is feeling more unsettled than the two girls sitting on their bed, Kate and Maggie.

....

It sounded just like this:
THUD THUD THUD THUD THUD THUD THUD THUD THUD THUD THUD THUD THUD THUD THUD THUD THUD THUD THUD THUD THUD THUD THUD THUD THUD THUD THUD THUD THUD THUD THUD THUD THUD.

I will never understand why adults insist on trying to keep ghost stories as a **grown-up thing** by telling kids they are too scary to read. It's completely unfair, because so many ghost stories have children at the heart of them, and, for this next case, we have not one but two rather remarkable young people.

Kate and Maggie Fox live in a tiny hamlet called Hydesville in Wayne County, New York, on the east coast of America. Which is where we've had to transport ourselves to using our super-duper teleportation powers. I hope you reset your watch to allow for the time difference?

···

That means **a village without a church**. *Interestingly, Shakespeare wrote a play about a Danish prince called* Hamlet, *and it features a ghost!*

When you think of New York, you're probably imagining giant skyscrapers, streets packed full of traffic and maybe even Teenage Mutant Ninja Turtles eating pizza. But where we are is **upstate New York**, the rural, countryside-y part of New York State, and when Kate and Maggie lived here it was mostly just farmland and small settlements. Because – I probably should have mentioned this earlier – we have also travelled back in time again. And this time, we have gone all the way to **1848**.

To get your head around exactly when that is, back in England, Queen Victoria has been on the throne for 11 years, and it's 31 years before Thomas Edison invents the electric lightbulb, so if you'd been alive then you'd have been reading this by candlelight.°

It's an era of many new discoveries. Cameras and bicycles had been invented, steam trains are taking over the world and there is a sense of amazement and wonder all across the globe about new breakthroughs in science. But that probably all feels a very long way away from the simple wooden farmhouse where

....

° *Though of course you couldn't have been reading it, because* **this book** *hadn't been invented yet.*

Kate and Maggie live with their mum and dad. The Fox family are poor. They are not the sort of people that special things happen to. But that's about to change in an enormous way ...

NEW YORK, NEW YORK ...

Yes, that's right, we have just travelled from York to **New York!** And since New York was actually named after the Duke of York by English settlers in 1664, it all feels pretty appropriate!

Did you know that before 1664, New York was called New Amsterdam, because it was controlled by Dutch settlers who had named it after their capital city, Amsterdam? You can probably see that the early settlers of America weren't very inventive when it came to naming places.

What shall we call it?

I know, let's use exactly the same name as the place we came from, but stick 'New' in front of it!

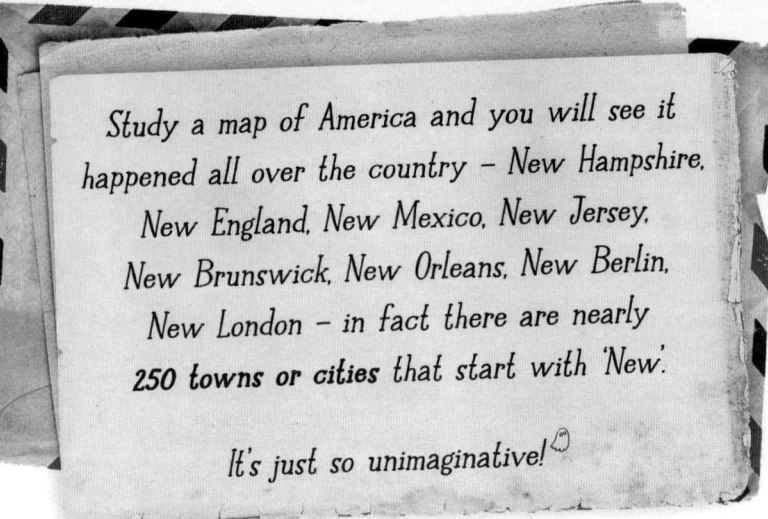

Study a map of America and you will see it happened all over the country – New Hampshire, New England, New Mexico, New Jersey, New Brunswick, New Orleans, New Berlin, New London – in fact there are nearly **250 towns or cities** that start with 'New'.

It's just so unimaginative!

Kate and Maggie are about to have their lives turned upside down. You see, this story is one of the BIGGEST in paranormal history. And if you thought Janet Hodgson in Enfield became famous from her haunting, wait till you see what happens to the Fox sisters. Their experience affected not just them and their family, but MILLIONS of other people too. In fact, by the end of it, the way almost everyone across the whole world felt about ghosts had completely changed, and it even led to the invention of a **whole new religion** that still exists today! Yes, you really did

....

My favourite American place names are: **Bigfoot**, *Texas;* **Bat Cave**, *North Carolina; and – best of all –* **Monkey's Eyebrow**, *Kentucky!*

read that right! How many people do you know who have successfully invented their own religion?

And it all started here in this bedroom on 31st March 1848. I often say to my own kids, 'If you have a problem, please tell me so I can try to help you fix it.' And that's exactly what the sisters did that day, emerging from their bedroom to tell their parents about the strange banging sound they said they could hear. Unfortunately, there was nothing Mr and Mrs Fox could do to stop it, and pretty soon **they** could hear it too.

THUD!
THUD!
THUD!

And the noises were not random – they seemed to respond to things Kate and Maggie said. So the

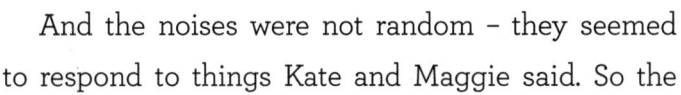

I tried to at school. I invented a religion called **Dannyanity** *and asked all my friends to worship me and offer me sacred gifts of crisps and fizzy drinks, but it didn't really catch on, sadly.*

This is good advice, even if I say so myself. Problems are like farts – they get worse and worse if you store them up. It's much better to get them out in the open.

girls agreed a code: 'Bang twice for yes and once for no', and asked questions.

'Who are you?'

'Why are you here?'

'Who is your favourite Teenage Mutant Ninja Turtle?'

(OK, they may not have asked that last one. Like electric lightbulbs, Teenage Mutant Ninja Turtles sadly hadn't been invented in 1848.) But Maggie and Kate do ask the first two questions and, astoundingly, after a flurry of further questions – rather like a ghostly game of Guess Who? – they learn that the invisible thing is the spirit of a **peddler** – that's a travelling salesperson – who was murdered and then buried under the Fox family's house. How spooky is that???

News of this shocking revelation spreads, which is why the neighbours come sniffing around, and why we find ourselves here, poking our own curious noses in. And using the magical power of being cartoon characters who can do anything we want, we are now going to go on a whistle-stop tour through the rest of Kate and Maggie's lives, experiencing everything they experience, as we fast-forward through what happens next. Because it's fair to say that things quickly get out of hand. After word gets round the neighbourhood about the 'spirit' who knows how old you are, crowds of local people start piling into the little farmhouse to gawp at these two young sisters who appear to have learned how to speak to a dead person.

Not everyone is impressed though. The minister in charge of the local church is so disapproving that he tells the Fox family to stop coming to services, and some local people wonder if the girls are actually witches, using magical powers to summon the spirit. Given all the attention, and the fact that the banging just won't stop, the family decide to move out of the farmhouse. I mean, you would, wouldn't you – if you discovered you had the ghost of a murdered person living under your floorboards?

Sadly, that doesn't do any good either, because – get this!!! – the noises *follow* Kate and Maggie!!!

O-M-blooming-G!!!!

Yes, it seems like wherever the Fox sisters go, the ghost follows, tapping and banging away, and after a

---

And you thought **mice** *were bad!*

while, it's not just the ghost of the peddler they're talking to – the girls can apparently summon pretty much any spirit they want on demand. So if someone asks if they might be able to make contact with his Auntie Mabel who passed away last year, a few moments later Kate and Maggie are chatting happily away with Mabel herself, passing on messages via their 'two for yes, one for no' code.

Which is a pretty useful skill to have, right? If you thought VHS tapes were revolutionary, what about an ability to dial up ANYONE who EVER lived from ANY period in history and ask them a question?

I'M A CELEBRITY GHOST – SPOOK ME OUT OF HERE!

If you could contact anyone from any period in history, who would you want to speak to? What would you ask them? It's a great question to consider and people have been trying to contact the spirits of famous historical figures for years. Here are three famous people who supposedly made contact from beyond the grave.

ELIZABETH I

One of our greatest-ever rulers, Elizabeth I was Queen of England from 1558 to 1603 – an incredible 45 years! And even after her death, it seems she may have kept an eye on how her beloved country was being run, checking in on other monarchs!

Both King George III and King Edward VII reportedly saw her ghost at Windsor Castle. In fact, **King George III** is said to have spoken with her! You might know that Elizabeth never married, but she apparently told George she was 'married to England'.

Another ruler, **King George VI**, the grandfather of our present-day King Charles III, claimed to have seen Elizabeth's ghost **eight nights in a row** at the outbreak of the Second World War!!! Was she appearing because she knew her country was in danger?

ABRAHAM LINCOLN

Abraham Lincoln was the American president back in the 1860s and was hugely influential in the abolition of slavery. Many Americans now consider him their greatest-ever president and his face is on the five-dollar banknote. But his face also appeared somewhere it wasn't expected when **Sir Winston Churchill**, the famous British prime minister who led the UK through the Second World War, visited the White House (the house where American presidents live).

Churchill was staying in one of the bedrooms there and had a habit of having a late-night bath while smoking a cigar. Legend has it that he got out of the bath and walked back into his bedroom completely naked (apart from his cigar), only to find the ghost of Lincoln standing by the fireplace!

Churchill – always cool in tough situations – said, 'Mr President, you seem to have me at a disadvantage!' and Lincoln apparently laughed and disappeared! It's probably one of the most embarrassing hauntings ever!

TUPAC SHAKUR

Tupac was a hugely well-known and successful rapper who was sadly shot and killed in a drive-by shooting in Las Vegas in America in 1996.

Some people think he was murdered because of arguments with rivals in the music business. He has continued to be a huge inspiration for a lot of young rappers, and one rapper in particular believes he actually had a message from Tupac's ghost!

You might have heard of Kendrick Lamar – he's now one of the biggest-selling hip-hop stars. Back when he was 21, he came home late from his recording studio to his mum's house and fell asleep on the sofa. He then had a dream where he was visited by the ghost of Tupac who told him: 'Keep doing what you're doing and don't let my music die.'

Was it just a dream? Or did Tupac really return from the dead to make sure Kendrick didn't give up on his music career?

The people of upstate New York couldn't be more excited once they had witnessed the Fox sisters' miraculous magical powers. There might be Victorian scientists beavering away trying to invent everything from electrical lights to telephones and radios in other parts of the world, but to the citizens of this small corner of eastern America, what Kate and Maggie can do feels like the **most amazing discovery** of their age.

And what do you do when you discover something amazing? You tell other people about it. Which is why we now find ourselves in a meeting hall in Rochester, the nearest big town to Hydesville. It's **14th November 1849**, and somebody has decided it was a good idea to book Kate and Maggie in here for a performance of their amazing contacting-the-dead skills.

We are sitting in an audience of **FOUR HUNDRED** people who have all bought tickets to watch the sisters speak to the spirits and answer the audience's questions! Can you imagine being on stage in front of that many people? It must be pretty nerve-wracking for Kate and Maggie, but I think you'll agree, the ghosts are truly impressive, doing everything from giving out advice on how best people should spend or save their money, to telling audience members who they should or shouldn't marry! I am impressed. It feels like the Victorian equivalent of asking Siri, 👻 and this is a historic day in paranormal history, because Kate and Maggie have just become the first people ever in the history of the world to charge money for being mediums.

Hold on ... I can see you have a question.

What's a medium?

👻 *I bet if you'd asked the ghost to tell you a joke containing the words wee, poo or bum, they would have done it too. That is how Siri is most often used in our house.*

I thought that one might come up. If you think it means someone whose clothes are between a small and a large, think again.

Well, OK, it does mean that, so technically you can still have a point for a correct answer, but a '**medium**' is also the name we give to someone who believes that they have a special ability to contact the dead and pass on messages to the living.

Before this performance in Rochester, there were people who claimed they had that power. But nobody has ever done it on this scale before, on stage in front of hundreds of people paying money for the privilege of watching.

Maggie and Kate are officially medium megastars! The closest thing we can compare it to is being a pop star, and after this show they find themselves touring around the country like a paranormal version of Taylor Swift or Beyoncé.

SEE THE FAMOUS
FOX SISTERS

SPEAK WITH THE
SPIRITS

BOOK YOUR TICKETS
NOW!

Their sister, Leah, becomes their manager, booking them into increasingly bigger and better venues. What started as a family haunting has now become a very successful **family business**, and as the sisters get written about in newspapers, their fame spreads, until it's not just upstate New York that is talking about them, but the whole world.

And you probably already know what happens when somebody is really good at something. Everybody else wants to be just like them! It's why kids dribble a ball to be like Leo Messi or dance around singing, mimicking Ariana Grande, or any other way you copy who your hero is. So, all over the globe, people decide they are also mediums and start contacting the dead too. Pretty soon, there are so many people interested in this amazing new form of 'spirit communication' that they get together in groups to do it and it becomes a fully-fledged religious movement called **Spiritualism**, where people meet in churches and try to contact the spirits of the dead together.

Wowsers. Kate and Maggie really have started something here. If we race forward through time again and watch the years go by, we can see

Spiritualism getting more and more popular. A big reason for this is that between 1861 and 1865, a terrible thing happened in America – the **American Civil War**. A civil war is where two armies from the same country fight each other, and, in this case, it was an army from the north of America, where Kate and Maggie live, fighting an army from the south. Almost 700,000 people are killed because of it. That is a lot of dead people, and those who are left behind – the parents, wives, sisters, brothers, friends and comrades of the dead soldiers – want to know if their loved ones are still out there somewhere in the afterlife. So lots of people become Spiritualists, and by the end of the 1800s there are Spiritualist churches all across America and eventually all over the world, filled with millions of people who are **totally and utterly confident** that the living can now speak with the dead.

Kate and Maggie have gone on quite a journey, from that simple wooden farmhouse to being

....

Abraham Lincoln *was president during the Civil War. He led the north to victory, but only five days after the war ended, he was shot dead by an assassin who supported the south.*

world-famous Spiritualist superstars. It is all rather wonderful. Except for one thing ...

None of it is true.

You'd better turn this page right now, because we have a LOT to talk about.

CHAPTER 8

A TOE-CURLING CONFESSION

In which we finally find out the truth about the not-so-fantastic Foxes and meet a famous writer who believes in fairies.

When I say 'None of it is true', I don't mean that everything we just experienced didn't actually happen. We know we stood in that bedroom listening to those **THUDS**, and we definitely sat in that hall in Rochester watching people throw their questions to the spirits and seemingly getting answers.

But Kate and Maggie were not being entirely honest about how they were doing it.

In fact, it seems they were completely and utterly lying to us all.

Because those noises in the house weren't coming from the ghost of a murdered peddler. Or from any ghost at all.

It was coming from **them**.

Perhaps we should remember the date when the noises first started – 31st March. The day before April Fools' Day, when people traditionally play pranks and try to trick others into believing things that aren't true.

You see, the whole story of the Fox sisters is probably the most successful April Fools' Day prank ever. Feeling bored, Kate and Maggie had decided to see if they could convince their parents that there was a ghost in the house, and it turned out they were just **too blooming good** at pretending.

Their parents completely believed it, and then, before the sisters really had time to think about the consequences of what they were doing, hundreds of other people believed it too and even wanted to pay them lots of money to display their 'superpowers'. And I think at that point it became way too hard to say it was actually all just a big joke that got out of hand, because a) you really don't want to disappoint hundreds of excited people and b) it's quite nice when people are giving you loads of money.

So when I said to you earlier, when we were in the sisters' bedroom listening to those **THUD THUD THUDS**, that Kate and Maggie were the most unsettled people there, it's because they were sitting, secretly making the noises themselves and slowly realizing they had become trapped by their own lie. And if you've ever had that feeling – where you know you're lying and that at some point you will be found out and things will be a hundred times worse – then you'll understand just how **tingly-tummy** uncomfortable that can be.

We are going to fast-forward to the end of the Fox sisters' story now, and – spoiler alert – it does not end happily, I'm afraid. As the years go by, Kate and

Maggie become grown-ups and they both drink too much alcohol, which is what adults sometimes do when they are unhappy and want to forget how they feel. But it doesn't work, and they just get unhappier, haunted by a ghost story they made up. They begin to appear drunk on stage. Nobody wants to see their performances any more, because there are other, better mediums around now. So the Fox sisters stop being cool like Taylor Swift, and become more like some really sad, uncool 90s pop band who can't get any concert bookings.[*] They go back to being poor, until one day a journalist from a newspaper offers them some money to finally tell the truth.

And so here we are in another big concert hall, the Academy of Music in New York City. It's **21st October 1888**, 40 years after we first heard those noises in Kate and Maggie's room, and a big audience has gathered again, only this time, people have come to hear them confess to being liars and frauds. Many sceptics had been convinced for a while that the sisters were secretly banging on the floor or walls early in the haunting to create the thuds in their

---

[*] *You know, one of those bands your parents like.*

house, but they couldn't understand how Kate and Maggie were able to produce noises on stage when everyone was watching.

The answer, revealed by Maggie to the packed theatre, is **truly ingenious**. She confesses that the girls have an unusual ability to crack the joints of their toes to make a loud clicking noise! So when they asked questions, it wasn't a ghost replying, but actually just their creaky big toes! How toe-tally dishonest!

A TOE-TAL FRAUD?

Kate and Maggie are not the only people to have been accused of faking a haunting with their toes! The same accusation was thrown at the witness in another famous paranormal case nearly 70 years later – the **Battersea Poltergeist**.

In the summer of 1956, many witnesses heard loud noises in a house in Battersea, South London, which was home to the Hitchings family. The sounds were so loud that they woke up the whole street! Just like Kate and Maggie, the family's teenage daughter, **Shirley Hitchings**, seemed to be able to communicate with the noises. Also like the Fox sisters, she became quite famous, appearing on TV and in newspapers.

But then, the **Daily Mail** newspaper published an article suggesting that Shirley had a special medical condition called 'hammer toe', which meant that her big toe made a loud clicking noise when she moved it, and she was using this to produce the sounds of the ghost.

It's an interesting theory, and for a while Shirley was discredited, but there were also lots of people who believed the Battersea Poltergeist haunting was completely genuine and wondered how any child's toe could make noises loud enough to **wake the neighbours up** next door.

There was also a lot of strange activity in the house that **definitely** can't be explained by deformed toe bones, like pots and pans flying across rooms and slippers seeming to walk around the house by themselves. Later in the case, there were some **truly amazing** moments, including messages apparently written by the poltergeist appearing on the walls, and even handwritten letters!

I made a podcast series about this haunting – if you're **feeling brave enough** you could listen to it to find out more. In the meantime, what do you think about the toe theory? Can **YOU** make a noise when you wiggle your toes? Does it sound like a ghost?

My jaw drops when I hear Maggie's confession in that concert hall. I don't know about you, but I feel completely duped. The scandalous truth behind their lies makes headlines in newspapers around the world. People never forgive the Fox sisters. No one likes to be tricked or taken advantage of. But I think what makes all the millions of people who read about it feel **most** angry is that they loved the idea of this remarkable, revolutionary invention – the ability to speak to the dead. And they absolutely do not want to be told that it was all a lie, concocted by two bored girls.

People want to believe. I know I do. It's why I get up every morning to investigate ghosts. It's maybe why you decided to read this book. We are excited and fascinated by the possibility that the paranormal could be real.

And so the Spiritualists just conveniently forget about the Fox sisters and carry on as normal. In fact, Spiritualism gets **even more popular**. It still exists now. If you search the internet, you might well find there is a Spiritualist church near you, where people still meet up and try and contact the dead to this very day.

SHERLOCK HOLMES AND THE SUPERNATURAL

One of the most famous believers in Spiritualism was Sir Arthur Conan Doyle, the author of the **Sherlock Holmes** detective stories. You might have heard of them – they were some of the bestselling stories of the late Victorian and Edwardian eras and are still hugely popular today, also made into TV series and films.

Sir Arthur was so passionate about Spiritualism that he toured around the world giving speeches about it. His interest in it was very personal. Both his son and his brother went to fight in the **First World War** and sadly died. Just like the American Civil War, the First World War caused a terrible loss of life, but this time right across the globe. So there were growing numbers of people like Sir Arthur who really wanted mediums to help them contact their lost loved ones.

Sir Arthur publicly supported lots of mediums, giving them his stamp of approval and getting into arguments with any sceptics who dared to suggest that the mediums' powers weren't real. He was also very interested in many other aspects of paranormal research and even found himself involved in a public debate about whether fairies were real after he saw some photographs taken by two girls in a village called Cottingley, near Bradford in north-west England. The photos seemed to show the girls playing in their garden with tiny fairies. If you google 'Cottingley fairies' you'll be able to see the photos – they became very famous!

Sir Arthur was convinced the photos were genuine, but eventually, when they were old women, the girls finally admitted they had **faked** them. One of the reasons they said they didn't confess at the time was because they didn't want to make Sir Arthur look stupid. So he definitely didn't get it right all the time! Was he right about Spiritualism? Is it really possible to receive messages from the dead?

Sadly, Sir Arthur died on **7th July 1930** from a heart attack, aged 71. On 13th July, the British Spiritualist Association booked the Royal Albert Hall, one of London's biggest concert halls, and an astonishing 10,000 people filled it to watch a medium called **Estelle Roberts** try to contact the spirit of Sir Arthur.

If his own ghost turned up, less than a week after his death, it would be the ultimate proof of everything Sir Arthur had believed! Sir Arthur's family were sat watching too, next to an **empty chair** – for him to sit in if he did appear.

The evening passed by with Estelle seemingly contacting several spirits who weren't Sir Arthur. But then suddenly she cried out, '**He is here!**' and described seeing Sir Arthur walking towards her. Estelle appeared to be listening to something he was saying. She leaned over to Sir Arthur's wife and said, '**The message is this. Tell Mary—**'

But at that point, the audience leaped up to applaud and the organist who was sat at the huge organ in the centre of the hall started to play loudly, **drowning out** what Estelle said and that was the end of the show!

Can you believe it?! To this day, nobody knows what Sir Arthur's message for Mary (his eldest daughter) actually was. So if you get annoyed at people talking over important bits of your favourite TV show, imagine how you would have felt about this, missing out on the crucial message that could have once and for all proved that ghosts exist!

Was Sir Arthur really communicating? Or could Estelle have been making the message up because she didn't want to disappoint people by not being able to make contact? **What do you think?**

#TeamSceptic –
if you'd been there, how would you have tested if what happened was genuine?

#TeamBeliever –
did 10,000 people witness a haunting?

I think you, me and Ellen need to learn from the sad story of Kate and Maggie, and from Sir Arthur's epic fairy-photo fail, and we should keep them in our heads as we carry on with our investigation.

Because we have confronted some confounding, convincing cases, but we still have some of the weirdest and most mysterious to come. We need to be very honest with ourselves. Does our desire to find paranormal answers stop us from seeing the facts clearly? If, like Sir Arthur, we really want ghosts to exist, is it more likely that we will find things that seem to prove they do? Remember when we learned about cognitive bias – how what you think can make you believe certain things? Well, your brain can also have confirmation bias, where you actually go out looking for things that confirm your theories and ignore things that don't.

I don't think I need to ask how you feel about the case of the fictitious, fantasizing, fraudulent Fox sisters, do I? I know which box you are going to tick.

....

Look back at pages 67–68 if you need to remind yourself and then meet me back here as quick as you can!

#TeamBeliever

#TeamSceptic

But **#TeamBeliever**, don't be downhearted. Because even though Kate and Maggie made things up, it doesn't automatically mean everyone else who's ever claimed to be able to contact the dead is lying. There have been many examples since 1848 where people have witnessed what do really seem to be strange messages from beyond the grave, and I have some BIG NEWS. We are about to explore a new case that is going to push **#TeamSceptic**'s theories to the very limit.

Because what if a ghost really did make contact . . . And then it got filmed on camera?

CHAPTER 9

THE
HAUNTED
TOILET

In which we face something far worse
than ghosts — the school toilets! We'll
also hear what scares Japanese children
and learn how to photograph a ghost.

It's a little unusual, I know, but I want to start this chapter with a theory.

#TeamBeliever *theory –*
What if ghosts are EVERYWHERE?

When I say 'everywhere', I mean literally **all over the place**. Huge crowds of them. Great long queues of everyone who's ever lived, from prehistoric times until now. Cavepeople, Romans, Vikings, medieval knights and peasants, Tudors, Victorians, suffragettes, Second World War soldiers, 1960s flower-power hippies and even people who died just last week – all hanging out together in a kind of afterlife.

And for some reason that scientists haven't discovered yet, very occasionally, a few of these people who used to live become visible to us for a brief, fleeting second. Like that moment on a grey day when the clouds suddenly part and you can see

---

*It would have to be a **pretty massive** afterlife, wouldn't it? If you added up everyone who has ever lived on Earth, then experts reckon it would be about 108 billion people. That's about 1.2 billion times the amount of people who can fit into Wembley Stadium. Even Taylor Swift doesn't get crowds like that!*

the Sun! Or when you watch a nature documentary and they go behind the scenes and you realize the camera team sat up a tree for three weeks just to catch a one-second glimpse of an exotic rare monkey doing a massive poop.

Let me explain how this might work with a handy Venn diagram I asked Ellen to draw:

Ghosts doing their thing

Living people doing our thing

HAUNTINGS!!!!!

I **REALLY** like this idea, because sometimes, when you read old books of ghost stories, it can seem like the only places that are haunted are ruined castles and historic stately homes. Or that all ghosts are dead kings and queens, or old-fashioned posh people

*What do you mean you've never watched a documentary about monkeys pooping? What are you **doing** with your life???*

who either died tragically or got their heads chopped off and then decided to come back as phantoms to scare tourists by walking through walls, rattling their chains and going

wooooooooOOOOOOooohhhhh!

But actually, wouldn't it make a lot more sense if EVERYWHERE in the world was haunted by ghosts who are just like us, hanging out, doing what regular humans do?

If we go along with this theory, perhaps you walked past some ghosts today on the street or in the supermarket. Perhaps, when you were in the park playing football, there was a group of ghosts having an invisible kick-about next to you. Maybe you even sat next to a ghost on the bus. That empty seat that felt oddly chilly . . .

I guess what I'm saying is, maybe every single day they are all around us – invisible, but there. And a haunting is when, by some amazingly exciting spooky-wooky one-in-a-million chance, one of these ghosts stops being invisible and we get lucky enough to see it. And there's no way you can control that; it's just at some completely random time in a completely random place that you will never expect.

Like a toilet.

You do want to hear about a haunted toilet, right?

Good. Then let me tell you about the night that **Stacey** thought she saw a ghost in the toilets at her school.

Stop right there.

I know what you're going to do.

You're going to say, 'DANNY, **ARE YOU CRAZY?** Kids don't go to school at **NIGHT!!!'** You mean one *DAY* at school.'

But Stacey is not a kid.

She's a cleaner. One of those nice, patient people whose job it is to come into school every night after you go home, to get rid of all the mess you leave

---

What did I tell you about **shouting?**

behind – the greasy fingerprints, dirty footprints, forgotten crisp packets and the yucky big green streaks from where you wipe your snot on the walls.👻

And she emailed me recently to tell me about a particular night a few years ago that she wanted me to help her investigate. So, having safely escaped 1840s America, let's dive back to **2013 Britain** and a secondary school in Castle Bromwich, near Birmingham, to follow Stacey as she does her rounds of the school corridors, wiping, polishing and mopping.

So far, so normal. But then, Stacey reaches the one place that she never likes going into.

You can probably smell it from here.

The boys' toilets.

Now you might think this is simply because the boys' toilets are the most wiffy, pongy, fart-tastic part of any school, which is usually true. But no, that is not the reason Stacey fears it.

Stacey doesn't like going in there because whenever she cleans the boys' toilets, she feels a very strong, overpowering sense of being watched. It's almost like there are eyes following her everywhere as she sprays and scrubs.

So she very reluctantly pushes the door open and does what she always does – checks the toilet cubicles, peers under the sinks and peeks behind the door. She even has a look in the locked cupboard where they keep the spare toilet rolls and paper towels ... but there is no one else here.

There never is. She is always alone. And yet, she can never quite shake off that **uncomfortable feeling**. She actually props open the door with her cleaning trolley today, just in case she decides she needs to make a run for it.

Which is silly, right?

It's just some empty toilets in a normal school on an ordinary night. This isn't *Jurassic World*, where a raptor is likely to burst out of a cubicle and try to bite your fingers off, or *Harry Potter*, where a Dementor might pop up next to the soap dispenser to steal your soul. It's not even a slightly lame YouTube prank video where some annoying dude jumps out and shouts '**you soooo totally got pranked, you loooooser, you are so skibidi!**'

There is literally nobody here. No one lurking in the dark, ready to shout . . .

BOO!!!!!!!!!!

Nothing to be scared of at all. But you can't always control how you feel, can you? And fear is one of the trickiest emotions. It sneaks into your head like a burglar and then won't leave. So Stacey cleans as quickly as she can, desperate for her shift to end so she can escape back home. There are just a few more jobs to do. First off, the disabled toilet. Let's follow her in.

If someone is reading this book to you and they didn't shout **'BOO'** *loud enough to make you jump, can you ask them to read it again louder? And if you are reading this yourself and didn't shout it out loud enough to make* **everyone else** *on your street jump, then you'd better read it again too!*

Scrub, scrub, scrub…

Spray, spray, spray…

Wipe, polish, wipe, polish…

Again, it all seems so normal, but Stacey can't get rid of that feeling. It's as if those eyes have followed her from one toilet to another. It makes the hair on the back of her neck stick up and a cold sweat break out on her forehead. And you know what? It's getting to me now too. I really do feel there is something else here, watching and waiting…

Phew. At last Stacey is finished! We follow her out and she closes the door. There's a handle and you have to pull it until it clicks to make sure the door is properly closed. Stacey does this and then spots some windows further down the corridor that are covered in greasy child fingerprints. She'll just give them a quick polish before she leaves –

But then…

CREEEE-AAAAKKKK …

We turn to look.

The disabled toilet door has opened itself!

Which is impossible.

To open that door, someone would have had to pull that handle Stacey just firmly closed, and, as I think we have well and truly established – there is **no one else here**.

But you and I know all too well from our previous adventures, when you are investigating ghosts, the impossible is never very far away. Here's another diagram from Ellen to show how that works:

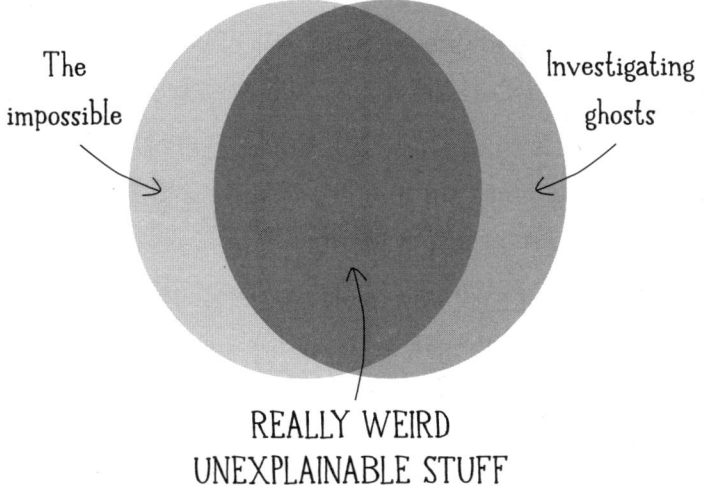

The impossible

Investigating ghosts

REALLY WEIRD
UNEXPLAINABLE STUFF

But would you have expected to find the impossible in your school toilets? Stacey certainly didn't, and she now decides it is about time to get the heck out of here. To be honest, I think she's got the right idea. This corridor is feeling distinctly chilly now, so let's follow her as quickly as we can towards the exit!

But just as we are making our getaway, there's another sound...

Something ominous . . . something sinister . . . something that feels to me like it is teetering right on the boundary between spooky and scary.

CLUMP, CLUMP, CLUMP, CLUMP ...

Footsteps.

Following behind us.

Footsteps down an empty corridor!

AAAAAAAAAAAARRGHHH!!!

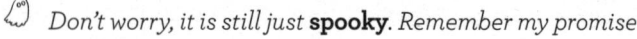

Don't worry, it is still just **spooky**. *Remember my promise!*

Stacey doesn't think she has ever been so frightened. An Olympic sprinter would have trouble catching up as she legs it out of the school as fast as she can, with us following, until she shoots off into the distance, running all the way home.

And as she climbs into bed that night, she tries really hard not to think about who or what those footsteps might have belonged to, tucking the whole incident away in that bit of her brain's filing system that is marked **TOTALLY WEIRD AND UNEXPLAINABLE**.

Until ...

A few days later, one of the school caretakers, who's in control of monitoring the CCTV security cameras that are set up around the school, asks Stacey and the other cleaners if they'd like to see something odd that was filmed on one of the cameras.

Can you guess which one?

The camera right by that toilet door.

Gulp. Stacey feels her neck prickle again at the thought of that night.

As the caretaker presses play on the video, you, me and Ellen creep up behind Stacey to watch the video too, looking on in fascination as she stands, gazing at the screen.

The video was filmed in the very middle of the night, long after the cleaners had gone home and long before the children and teachers came in the next morning. It's the time that writers and poets sometimes call the '**dead of night**', when all is quiet and cold and lonely, the darkness is at its darkest and there is certainly nobody walking around a school.

Nobody human at least.

Which is what makes this video all the more surprising, because, as we watch the grainy image of the corridor, illuminated by the camera's night-vision mode, we see . . .

The toilet door opening by itself!

(Remember we worked out that was impossible!)

And inside the toilet . . .

The light switches on!

(Also impossible.)

And in the doorway of the toilet is . . .

A MAN!

(Did I mention this was all utterly IMPOSSIBLE?)

A **BIG** shiver runs down Stacey's spine, like a rollercoaster of tense, trembling, trepidatious tingles.

Could it be a thief who snuck in and needed a wee? Or a teacher who fell asleep in a classroom and has now got up for a night-time poo?

But then, any possibility that this could be a real living, breathing, weeing and pooing human being is gone, because the man **LITERALLY DISAPPEARS** *IN FRONT OF STACEY'S EYES!!!!!* (OK, this is getting crazy now – how much more impossible do you want???)

And to Stacey, at that moment, it seems very likely that the toilet where she felt so strange, where she saw a door open itself and heard footsteps following her, is actually, definitely … **haunted**.

GHOSTS CAUGHT ON CAMERA?

Did Stacey really see a video of a ghost?
One question I am often asked is why don't more
hauntings get captured on video? After all, we live
in a time where almost every adult in the world
has a camera with them everywhere they go – on
their smartphone. So, if people are really seeing
what they think are ghosts, why aren't they
photographing or filming them?

Well, the short answer is: they
are. On the internet, especially
on sites like TikTok and Reddit,
there are loads of people who
claim they've managed to film
potential paranormal activity
and post videos of it. But
there is one big problem.

No one trusts or believes them.

It's not their fault. It's because of another modern invention that we humans have come up with. AI. Or to give it its full name, 'Artificial Intelligence'.

AI programs allow people to alter and even completely fake video footage. The technology is so clever now that people are able to produce videos of celebrities talking, moving around and doing things that seem so authentic that when you watch it you are convinced it is the real person – even though you know what they are saying or doing can't be true, like making the Arsenal football manager say he really likes Tottenham or making the prime minister breakdance to hip-hop music.

BEEP!

So in a world where we know computer technology can very literally show us the impossible, can we ever trust what we see? Is that really a video or photo of poltergeist activity, or something that's been cooked up cleverly using AI software to deceive us?

It's a big problem to anyone trying to work out if ghosts are real. Because, obviously, if we really could catch a ghost on camera, it would go a long way towards proving their existence. Personally, I'd love to believe that we might one day capture a definite ghost sighting on film! If you ever get to investigate a haunted house, take a camera with you and see what you can film while you're there!

But let's get back to Stacey, because when her email popped into my inbox asking for help in trying to make sense of things, it really got my attention.

What happened seemed pretty incredible, but I was also very interested in *where* it happened. Because you might think a school toilet is the last place you'd expect to meet a ghost, but you know what? Stories about haunted school toilets and bathrooms are actually a lot more common than you might think!

In Britain, there is a popular urban legend 👻 – **'The Green Lady of the Toilet'** – about a lady dressed

....

👻 *An urban legend is a story that has been told so many times by so many different people over such a long period of time that nobody knows if it is true or not any more.*

in green who is said to haunt school toilets, and many children in the UK and America will be familiar with the **'Bloody Mary'** game – the idea that if you look in the mirror and say 'Bloody Mary' three times a ghostly spirit called Bloody Mary will appear. It's Japan, though, that for some reason, seems to have the most stories about ghosts who haunt toilets and bathrooms.

There are absolutely LOADS of them, including one about a spirit called **Aka Manto**, who hangs out in the toilets in a red cloak and mask offering unsuspecting people a choice of red or blue toilet paper, which is nicely weird. But my personal favourite Japanese toilet ghost story is about a spirit called **Hanako-san**, who is said to be the ghost of a young girl who died while playing hide-and-seek during an air raid in the Second World War.

To summon her, you have to knock three times on the door of the third cubicle of the third-floor toilets at your school (I'm not sure what you're meant to do if your school doesn't have three floors!). Once you have knocked, you ask Hanako-San if she is there and she will appear! Then, depending on which version of the story you get told, she will either pull you down the toilet (pretty smelly) or you will be eaten by a three-headed lizard (a *lot* worse).

Now, I hope it goes without saying that all these stories are just made-up fairy tales, often told by older kids to spook out younger ones and make them scared to go to the loo at school. You don't need to actually worry about Hanako-San, she doesn't exist. But sometimes fairy tales are based on a grain of truth and are a way for humans to try and make sense of things we have experienced, and, judging by the number of emails I receive about **toilet hauntings**, it does seem like there are a lot of people out there who've been spooked on the loo.

Over the years, I've had emails about toilets with strange noises, strange feelings, strange ghostly apparitions and even a few emails about toilets that seem to mysteriously flush themselves!

So it's time for you, me and Ellen to regroup in Stacey's school loo, and try to figure out what is going on there.

Is there really something about toilets that makes them more likely to be haunted?

What kind of a ghost would want to hang out somewhere so stinky?

Or can we **flush away** these phantoms by explaining them scientifically?

These are the questions we need to consider as we pit our sceptic theories against our believer theories, to see if we can crack this bizarre bathroom baffler.

I'll see you in there!

....

*Perhaps it is a **poo**-tergeist?*

CHAPTER 10

THE FEAR YOU CAN'T HEAR

In which we learn how to escape a roaring tiger, meet a sword-wielding scientist and hear how a toilet flush might be hiding something fantastic.

I'll let you sit on the loo and I'll stand. I agree it's not the most comfortable place to try and crack a case, but this toilet is the scene of the supernatural crime, so we should keep our eyes peeled for any clues as we discuss our theories. And boy oh boy, do I have a couple of absolute crackers for you! Let me write them down on this handy bit of toilet roll.

#TeamSceptic theory –

Infrasonic vibrations!

Listen very carefully. Can you hear that? No, of course you can't, because it's **infrasound!**

Let me explain . . . We measure sounds using something called hertz. Human beings can only hear sounds that sit within a range of 20 to 20,000 hertz.

Sounds above 20,000 hertz are called '**ultrasound**'. One example of this is a dog whistle – it's so high-pitched that we can't hear it, but dogs can because they have a greater hearing range than us.

On the other end of the scale, 'infrasound' is the word used to describe sounds below 20 hertz and, although we may not be able to hear it, scientists do think infrasound can have a big effect on us.

In particular, infrasound that hits the 19 hertz frequency is believed to create feelings of anxiety or even fear. People sometimes call it 'the fear you can't hear'. I did an experiment once where I was exposed to infrasound and I can confirm it really does make you feel **deeply weird**. It gives you a strange feeling in the pit of your stomach and makes your whole body feel twitchy and uncomfortable.

....

*It's pronounced '***hurts***'. And did you know, if you hear too many hertz, it hurts!*

Dogs can hear up to 60,000 hertz. Their sensitive hearing is also why they get frightened by fireworks.

Interestingly, infrasound at 19 hertz is actually present in a **tiger's roar**. It helps the tiger hunt by creating a sense of fear that can literally paralyse its prey! So if you ever come face-to-face with a tiger, put your hands over your ears quick so you can't hear its roar and try and get out of there before the 'fear frequency' traps you, ready for the tiger to gobble you up!

Some experts also believe that infrasound can lead people to feeling a sense of presence, like they are

This is advice you will probably never have to use. You might have read the book The Tiger Who Came to Tea *but I am afraid to say it is not based on truth. Tigers almost never come to tea at British houses.*

being watched, and that it can even potentially create a **vibration of your eyeballs** that could make you hallucinate figures or shapes! Listening to all that, can you see why sceptics think infrasound could be a possible reason why some people believe they are being haunted?

But how could it be linked to Stacey's case? Surely there is no infrasound in a school toilet? In the UK, the chances of a tiger leaping out at you from a toilet cubicle are pretty slim, even at the toughest schools. But could infrasound actually be present in a way you might never have expected?

The first person to really explore how infrasound might be linked to ghost experiences was a man called **Vic Tandy**.

Back in the **early 1980s**, Vic was working in a laboratory designing medical equipment. Some rumours had started among the other staff that the laboratory was haunted, and one evening, while Vic was working in the lab late on his own, he began to feel uncomfortable. In fact, it

was a feeling very similar to the one Stacey described in the boys' toilets. The hair stood up on the back of Vic's neck, he felt a cold sweat on his forehead and he was totally convinced that he was being watched. Then, out of the corner of his eye, Vic saw a strange grey shape float into view! When he turned around to confront it, it had disappeared!

Just like Stacey, Vic was utterly terrified and decided to get out of there as fast as he could! Had he experienced the laboratory ghost?

The next day, when Vic went into work, he took a sword with him – not because he was planning to use it to fight off the ghost, but because he was a keen amateur fencer (that's the sport of sword fighting, not someone who puts up garden fences!). He needed to do some repairs to his sword – a particularly thin-bladed type called a **'foil'** – and so he clamped it into a vice. But, while he was doing his repairs,

---

Though that would have been **pretty cool**. I am already planning my next book – Scientists Who Sword-Fight Spirits.

That's a type of clamp on a workbench that holds things tight while you are working on them! Though 'vice' can also be an old-fashioned word for a bad habit. Funnily enough, it's a **vice** to try and put your fingers into a **vice**!

he noticed that the sword was vibrating up and down very fast.

This struck him as strange. Why was it doing that?

With a little bit of detective work, he was able to work out that the vibrations were due to sound waves that were being produced by a new **extractor fan** that had been installed in the laboratory. The sound wasn't audible – it was infrasound. He switched the fan off and the sword stopped vibrating!

And just like that, Vic had solved the mystery of the haunted laboratory. Nobody had reported any haunting experiences before the fan was installed and nobody reported any after it was turned off, so Vic was able to deduce that it was the infrasound that was causing him and the rest of the staff to imagine a ghostly presence.

All of this feels very interesting for our case, doesn't it? Because not only do the feelings Vic reported sound almost identical to what Stacey felt, but we know the one thing all school toilets are likely to have is a **bad smell**, and what do you need to get rid of a smell?

An extractor fan.

Could all of these **toilet hauntings** be explained by the inaudible hum of a fan?

What do you think? Are you a *fan* of this theory?

So the sceptics have had their say, and it is an impressive theory, I'll give them that. But hang on just a moment here while we look at the evidence in this case . . .

Infrasound might explain some of the feelings Stacey had, but it doesn't explain a toilet door impossibly opening itself, the sound of footsteps following her down an empty corridor, or a toilet light switching itself on at night when no one else is in the school. And it categorically certainly absolutely **does not explain** a man appearing and disappearing, all recorded on video!

There is definitely more to this case than can be explained away by infrasound! So could the answer lie in something else that is present in every toilet across the land?

Water.

....

What do you mean, that's another terrible dad joke? I'd been working on that one for **ages!**

#TeamBeliever
theory –

Something in the water

You weren't expecting me to say that, were you? But there are some ghost hunters who believe that the presence of **water** at a location might be linked to the appearance of ghosts. Many hauntings seem to take place on the site of underground rivers or lakes, and those who believe in this theory wonder if paranormal energy can somehow be transported by water.

It sounds fantastical, but could they be on to something?

Well, I should probably tell you about a French medical scientist called **Jacques Benveniste**, who conducted a series of experiments in the late 1980s – not that long after Vic Tandy was fixing his 'haunted' fan. Jacques was studying why people have **allergic reactions** and how it can be linked to a type of blood cell called a basophil. Jacques knew that allergic reactions occur when someone's basophils come into contact with

an allergen (that's a substance they're allergic to – such as wheat, shellfish or milk). He had come up with a way to test basophils by adding a dye to them, so that when they came into

contact with an allergen, they turned blue.

Jacques spent lots of time testing this, mixing different allergens with water, and then adding basophils and watching them go blue when they reacted.

But then the experiment went wrong – and some people think that what happened might help us answer our paranormal questions!

Basically, one of Jacques' helpers had messed things up and over-diluted a substance until the solution was *only* water – there was no allergen left. But when they introduced the basophil, it still turned blue! It was somehow reacting to an allergen that was no longer there!

The team were completely confused, so they repeated the experiment in the same way hundreds of times. The water always reacted in the same way!

What it seemed to show was something truly remarkable – that water molecules have a 'memory'. They appear to 'record' the substances they have been in contact with.

So some paranormal investigators now wonder whether water could also record sounds and images in this way. Remember we talked about Stone Tape Theory on page 84? I guess this is **Water Tape Theory**.

Could Stacey's ghost have been produced by the water running in the sink? Could a flush have unleashed her phantom that ended up on film?

It's quite a thought, isn't it? That the substance we all take for granted, splash around in when we're having a bath, swig from a glass on a hot day and use to flush away our poos and wees, might actually remember details about us.

It's time to vote. As ever, there are no right or wrong answers here, just your opinion. So weigh up the evidence and decide if you are:

 **#TeamBeliever**

#TeamSceptic

Right, now that's settled, I think it's high time we got out of these toilets. I don't know about you, but I'm getting a bit hungry and I did promise your parents I would regularly feed you. Perhaps we should go and find those posh chocolate biscuits we stole from the RAF canteen –

RING RING RING RING

Sorry, I think that's my phone. I know this is very rude, but if you'll excuse me, I'd better **answer it** in case it's important.

Hello?

...

Yes, this is 'that ghost-hunter bloke'.

...

*Oh **really?***

...

*That is **very** interesting.*
Very interesting indeed.
I'll be with you as soon as I can.

...

*Can I bring some **chocolate biscuits?***
Yes, of course I can!

Sorry – normally I'd have let it go to voicemail, and also, there may be one less chocolate biscuit now, because that was a really important call. It came from 1977 and it was our old friend Graham Morris, the *Daily Mirror* photographer we met in Enfield, the one who got hit by the flying LEGO brick. Remember he said he'd tip us off if anything else happened in Janet's case? Well, it turns out something *very* strange indeed has just occurred – something **so odd** that Graham is going to need a biscuit to help him recover.

So grab that packet from my rucksack and let's take some more deep breaths. It's time to travel back once again to 284 Green Street and the 1970s. And if you thought the idea of capturing a ghost on camera was interesting, just wait until you see the photo Graham has taken.

It will shock you.

It will **spook** you.

It might even make you believe in ghosts.

CHAPTER 11

CAN CHILDREN FLY?

In which we pay a flying visit to Enfield, hear a shockingly spooky recording and very nearly injure my own children.

We are in Janet's bedroom. If I'm honest, I'm not very keen on her wallpaper or carpet, but **this is the 1970s** and people had very different taste back then. She shares the room with her sister, Margaret, and just like you, they've got posters of some of their favourite things on the wall – pop stars and TV actors. It's really a very normal bedroom for two nearly teenage girls, but, as we learned on our first visit here, what's been happening in the Hodgson family home is far from normal. And I'm afraid to say things have been getting even weirder since we left!

Let me bring you up to date on the investigation – there is now a team of ghost hunters here camping out at the house. They have come from a group called the **Society for Psychical Research**. They're paranormal experts who have been studying the poltergeist phenomena with special equipment and making tape recordings to try to work out what is going on.

And one of these tape recordings is . . . well, let's just say listening to it made me go completely **cold and tingly**, as if a spooky, ghostly finger had just tickled my neck.

In the recording, the ghost hunters are talking to Janet, asking her questions, and she is replying –

only she's not replying with her own voice! The voice that comes out of Janet's mouth is deep and gruff, and claims to be an **old man** who calls himself Bill.

The ghost hunters wonder if Janet has become 'possessed' by a ghost, who has taken over her vocal cords, speaking through her to talk to them. Which is a pretty wild idea, right?

And then, something even freakier happened.

Oh blimey, I can feel my knees trembling as I tell you about this. In fact, even my toes are shaking when I think about it. You see, our photographer friend Graham has been helping the ghost hunters, taking photos of whatever strange activity he can catch on camera.

....

*They are **not** making noises, though, like the Fox sisters' toes. If they did make noises, I'd probably teach them to play a tune. Maybe something by **Toe-ler Swift**. Get it?*

Which is easier said than done.

I mean, you might think you're good at taking photos on your parents' phones, but you just try having it ready to go at the exact precise moment a poltergeist decides to throw something across a room. It's not easy!

So Graham has mostly been taking photos of the *after effects* of what happens – scenes of disruption and chaos when the poltergeist cheekily decides to rearrange some furniture.

But last night, that changed – in a **BIG** way. Graham managed to photograph the EXACT moment that the poltergeist seemingly threw something across Janet's bedroom.

And that **something** was . . . ?

Have a guess . . .

A plate?

A cup?

A slipper?

A teddy bear?

A pillow?

No. No. No. No. And no. Any other guesses?

Another LEGO brick?

Still no.

Some smelly old socks?

No!!!

I'm just going to have to tell you, aren't I?

The thing thrown across Janet's bedroom was . . .

Janet.

Yes, the potential paranormal activity at 284 Green Street has definitely got a lot worse because it seems that the Enfield Poltergeist, as all the newspapers are now calling it, has just hurled an 11-year-old girl across her bedroom!!!

Now, firstly, let me reassure you. Janet is OK. She screamed as it happened, but she wasn't injured and is feeling fine now. But holy moly, do we have some incredible evidence to consider, because the amazing thing is that Graham managed to **photograph** it as it happened. Can you believe that? And I'm going to show you the photograph right now.

Don't worry, it's not a scary picture. But it is quite surprising, so I think you should make sure you're sitting down comfortably when you look at it. Or, if you're reading this in bed, you might want a nice squishy pillow nearby that you can give a little squeeze while you say, 'Oh my goodness me, I did not expect to see that!'

So, if you are ready, on the count of three, we're going to turn the page and look at the photo together.

One.

Get ready!

Two.

Don't chicken out ...

Three.

Let's do this!!!

*TURN
THE
PAGE*

NOW*!!!!!!!!!!!!!!!!!!!!!!!!!!!!!!*

See what I mean?

As you can probably see, it's Janet's bedroom
(didn't I tell you the wallpaper and carpet were a bit
yucky?). There are the posters on the wall, and there,
in the middle of the picture, it is very clear that Janet
is being **thrown across the room** by an invisible
paranormal force.

Or is it?

Because since Graham took the photo, quite a few
sceptics have come up with a different theory for
what happened.

They think this photo shows Janet jumping off her bed.

So I want you to look at it again with this other theory in your mind.

Study it really closely.

What does that look on Janet's face tell you?

Because I was convinced it was **fear and shock** – a child who definitely did not expect to be picked up by a ghost and thrown across her bedroom.

But could it actually be someone *pretending* to feel like that as she jumps as high as she can off her bed?

How are you feeling about it right now?

 # TeamBeliever

TeamSceptic

It's really tricky to decide, isn't it? I want to believe Janet when she says that it really happened, but I also know that children (and even adults too) sometimes get carried away and do things they shouldn't, just to get attention. So, what do you reckon – is this a haunting or a hoax?

THE ENFIELD GHOST HUNTERS

If Janet was faking things, then the people whose attention she was trying to get were the two ghost hunters who came and stayed with the family to investigate the case. Their names were Maurice Grosse and Guy Lyon Playfair, and they were part of the **Society for Psychical Research** – often simply shortened to the **SPR**.

The SPR is the **oldest ghost-hunting group** in the world. It was set up in 1882 by a group of Victorians who were fascinated by the paranormal and wanted to study it. Sir Arthur Conan Doyle, who we met earlier, was an early member, and many of the other people who joined were scientists or writers who devoted their free time to conducting paranormal experiments, many of which involved testing mediums to see if they were genuine.

After a while, the Society developed a reputation as somewhere that people could write to if they felt their house was haunted. Investigators from the SPR would come out **free of charge** and spend time studying the haunting to see if there was anything they could do to help. This still happens today and the SPR has incredible records of all the hauntings it has ever investigated.

The SPR became involved in the Enfield Poltergeist case after the **Daily Mirror** newspaper contacted them. They sent Maurice and Guy to investigate and the pair spent a huge amount of time at the house with the Hodgson family.

But some people, including the more sceptical members of the SPR, worried that Maurice and Guy were perhaps so excited about the possibility of proving that the haunting was genuinely paranormal that they ignored potential sceptic explanations.

Some other experts also came to investigate at the house, including a **ventriloquist** called Ray Allen. You might not have heard of a ventriloquist[⬤] before – they are not as common as they used to be. It's someone who performs a stage act where they appear to make a puppet talk. It's actually the ventriloquist talking, but they have cleverly learned a way to project their voice without moving their lips![⬤] Ray Allen was one of the most famous ventriloquists back at the time of the haunting. He had a puppet called Lord Charles. You can see videos of them performing together on YouTube and it really is amazing. Ray's lips don't move at all, but Lord Charles speaks! The reason Ray was invited to the house was to witness Janet talking with the old man's voice and give his professional opinion as to whether she might also have learned how to do ventriloquism and if the old man's voice could be Janet putting on a deep voice and then seeming to speak without moving her lips. Do you think that could be a possible explanation for what happened?

....

It's not an easy word to say. Or spell!

'Ventriloquist' is even harder to say without moving your lips!

Ray said he thought Janet might be faking the voice, but then, years later, when Maurice Grosse appeared on a radio show and played a recording of Janet speaking in the old man's voice, a man phoned the radio show to say that **he recognized it!** The man said it was the voice of his dad, who had lived and died at 284 Green Street, and that his dad's name was . . . **Bill!** Hearing that sends a shiver down my spine. What do you think about it?

Maurice Grosse and Guy Lyon Playfair are both dead now, so we can't ask them what they think of the photograph of Janet flying, but they always maintained that they believed that the haunting was genuine. They felt they had witnessed too many things with their own eyes that could not possibly be explained.

The Society for Psychical Research still exists today. You have to be over 16 to join, but maybe one day you can become a member and help them investigate ghosts. Perhaps you'll find a case just as intriguing as the Enfield Poltergeist!

But back to the photo. Surely there's an easy way to sort this mystery out – we can just ask the person who took it. Graham will be able to tell us exactly what he saw in that bedroom, won't he?

Except we have one big problem.

Graham wasn't there.

WHAT???

I know what you're thinking – how can someone not be there to see something happen if they have just taken a photo of it? Surely that is even more impossible than a toilet door opening itself?

Well, here's how it happened ... Since Graham and the ghost hunters were at Janet's house so much, Graham had decided it was important to make Janet and her family's life still feel as normal as possible. After all, it would be pretty annoying if he was always camped out in her bedroom with his camera. So, he came up with a way of taking **remote-operated photos** – where he could leave his camera in a room but he didn't need to be there himself. I'll let him explain ...

'I had a **switch**, and we would sit downstairs and listen to live audio from Janet's bedroom through the tape recorder from the Society of Psychical Research guys and, if I heard something, I would just press the switch and the camera would take photos!

'So, on this particular night, we were sat downstairs. The kids had gone to bed, it was quiet, you could hear sort of murmurings and the girls chatting to each other, and then they finally went to sleep. And then . . .

CRASH! BANG! SCREAM!

So I hit the button and the camera took pictures!'

Which is great – thanks, Graham – except it means we are still none the wiser about what this photo actually shows! Flying girl or faking girl?

I think there's only one way to discover the truth.

We need to do an **experiment**.

For this, we're going to need a bedroom and a child to throw across it.

Now, I would ask **you** to help, but I've been told by the people who publish this book that your parents won't be too happy if you get injured while reading it. Apparently encouraging children to do dangerous stunts is discouraged these days. Which seems pretty booooooooring to me, but I have to keep to the rules. So, instead of using you, I am going to use my own children instead.

I'd like you to meet my sons, Leo and Max.

Well, OK, it's the **cartoon versions** of them. Leo is 12 and Max is 9. They both support Arsenal and like *Star Wars* and they sometimes argue with each other, though most of the time they get on pretty well. Which is good, because I am now going to ask them to work as a team as we transport ourselves from 1970s Enfield to **present-day Walthamstow** in East London, where I live, and head upstairs in my house to Leo and Max's bedroom.

It has their names written on the door and inside they have lots of posters on the wall, just like Janet and Margaret. Leo and Max's posters are mostly of footballers and stormtroopers rather than 1970s pop stars, but it's still pretty similar to Janet's room, which I think is important, as we need our experiment to be as authentic as possible if we're to have any hope of proving what might have gone on the night Graham took the photo. So, without any further ado, let's get started, shall we?

Danny: *'Right, Leo and Max, I need you to concentrate. We have a job to do.'*

Leo: *'OK, Dad. And who's that* **kid** *in the white sheet?'*

Danny: *'Oh, that's the person reading this book right now. I think you'd like them – they seem pretty cool.'*

Leo: *'Oh, OK. Hi there, reader! Do you like Star Wars?'*

Danny: *'We don't have time to talk about Star Wars, Leo!*  *We need to conduct an important* **scientific experiment***.'*

Max: *'What do we need to do?'*

Danny: *'Well, Max, I basically want you to throw yourselves through the air.'*

Max: *'You mean throw the cartoon versions of ourselves that Ellen just drew?'*

Leo: *'Why did Ellen draw them, Dad? Why not you? Is it because you are* **reeeeally bad** *at drawing?'*

👻 *Though did you know that the first* Star Wars *film came out in 1977 – the same year that the Enfield Poltergeist haunting started?*

186

Danny: *'What? I'm not bad at drawing! I got her to do them because I'm too busy writing this book and investigating ghosts, OK? Don't be cheeky. And no, Max, I don't mean throw the cartoon versions of you. We are going to throw the* **actual real-life** *versions of you.'*

Max: *'Sounds a bit dangerous!'*

Danny: *'Don't worry! All I need you to do is jump up and down on your bed as high as you can while I try to take photographs.'*

Leo: *'That sounds a bit weird. What does* **Mum** *think about this?'*

Danny: *'She . . . erm . . . thinks it's a good idea.'*

Leo: *'Have you asked her?'*

Danny: *'Erm . . . kind of . . .'*

Leo: *'Are you lying?'*

Danny: *'Maybe.'*

Max: *'Why are we doing this?'*

Danny: *'Because I want to test out a theory. There's this photo of a girl called Janet and it looks like she is being thrown across the room by a poltergeist...'*

Max: *'What's a* **poltergeist?***'*

Danny: *'We don't have time to explain that either! Can you just go back and read pages 18–21, please? There's a really well-written explanation of poltergeists, even if I say so myself. Basically, they cause trouble and throw stuff around.'*

Leo: *'Like Max?'*

Max: *'Oi! Don't you say that about me!!!'*

Danny: *'Boys,* **stop fighting!!!** *We are getting distracted here. In the photo it really does look like Janet is flying, but I want to know, would it be possible to take a photo like that if she was only jumping up in the air?'*

Leo: *'So you basically want us to try and recreate the photo to see if it could be faked?'*

Danny: *'Bingo! Are you ready? I'll get my camera ready. You start **jumping** … NOW!!!!'*

And so, for the next five minutes, Leo and Max jump up and down on their bed.

BOING BOING BOING

And I take photos.

CLICK CLICK CLICK

And, while it is pretty fun watching two children jump up and down repeatedly, I think we should probably fast-forward to the end of the experiment – for safety reasons if nothing else. I forgot that Leo and Max have a bunk bed, and jumping on the top bunk, Leo very nearly just put his head through the ceiling. So I think it is time to wrap things up and assess our evidence. And when I say '**evidence**', yes I do mean some quite bad, wobbly photos I took on my phone.

Here they are . . .

CLICK!

I know, I'm as bad at taking photos as I am at drawing. But what I think it proves is that it's **really hard** to capture that moment when someone is up in mid-air. They're already coming down by the time you've even clicked the button to take the photograph.

Now flick back a few pages and have another look at that photo of Janet suspended in the air. Could that picture really have been taken if she was just **jumping?**

The other thing our experiment proved was that children giggle a lot while jumping. And look again at Janet's expression on her face. It really does look like **fear**, doesn't it? Could she have faked that?

The one thing we can say for certain is that we will never have a definite answer, and, in a way, the photo of Janet sums up the problem we will always have as paranormal investigators.

Hauntings happen to somebody else.

Unless something is actually happening directly to you, all you can ever try to do is interpret the evidence, decide if you believe that person, consider whether they could have become confused and misinterpreted what happened, and then take all of your thoughts and feelings and use them to come up with some theories.

That's what I have been trying to teach you to do. And I think we've done it well. We've had some fantastic theories – RSPK, Stone Tape Theory, infrasound, the memory of water, noisy toes . . .

But they are all just theories.

We can never know for sure
what happened in each of these cases
because we weren't inside the head of
the person who was experiencing it – we can't
know what they saw through their eyes,
what they heard, what they felt.

The only way to ever 110% verify if a haunting is genuinely paranormal would be to experience it **yourself**, right?

So, I think it's finally time for me to tell you about the night I spent in a haunted house. And you might want to take another big deep breath or two, because things are about to get very, very spooky.

What do you mean the maximum you can get is 100%? Who are you – my maths teacher?

CHAPTER 12

A NIGHT IN A HAUNTED HOUSE

In which we get very wet putting up a tent, hang out in one of Britain's most haunted houses and meet a polar explorer with a ghostly friend.

Darkness is falling.

It's raining hard. Big nasty drops, determined to drench us to the bone. The weather report is warning that a massive gale-force wind is brewing and, suddenly, the idea of camping in a potentially haunted house in the middle of the Scottish Highlands doesn't feel like quite so great an idea. Especially this particular haunted house, which is so old and ruined it doesn't even have a roof. So, I've got just a flimsy tent to protect me from the fearsome Scottish weather and also anything spooky that might be lurking here in the dark ...

'Do you believe in ghosts?' I ask Phil, who is standing next to me, trying to put up his own tent by the light of his head torch as rain trickles down the backs of our waterproof jackets.

LUIBEILT

'Oh yes,' he says. **'Definitely**. Because of what happened to me in this house. And hopefully, after tonight, Danny, you'll believe too.'

And so here we are.

What a journey you and I have been on together over the last eleven chapters. It's taken us across the UK and even to America, and through more than one century. We've met 1970s London children, Roman soldiers, Victorian mediums, spoon-bending magicians, sabre-toothed tigers, phantom Second World War pilots, Japanese toilet ghosts, a ghoulish Elizabeth I, a naked Winston Churchill, the Brown Lady of Raynham Hall, and, most terrifyingly of all, my own kids.

But it all ends here, in this remote ruin poking out of the rain-lashed Scottish landscape like a rotten tooth.

If I'm honest, when we started out on our quest back in chapter one, I was worried.

I knew you were brilliant and clever, but I was concerned you might get, well . . . a bit spooked out. After all, the paranormal is a strange business, and we have investigated some of the oddest hauntings of all time. But, throughout it all, you've stood firm, never running off screaming,

'HEEEEEELP MEEEEEE!!!!!!!! GET MEEEE OUUUUT OF HEEEEEEEEEERE!!!!'

And you've even managed to keep that **bedsheet** on the whole time without getting too sweaty. I'm impressed.

And I realize you're not just clever and brilliant, you're also brave. Perhaps it's not just ghosts you can face up to now.

....

*If perhaps occasionally snotty and **farty**.*

The next time you encounter something that might have previously made you feel anxious or even scared, you can think back to some of the things we have learned together, like why humans have a fear of the dark, or why we think we see the shapes of people lurking in corners, and you'll remember that our brains can sometimes be a little annoying and malfunction, telling us to be scared of things when really we don't need to be. But also, that the best way to deal with anything you find scary is to **talk about it** with someone who you trust.

You see, ghosts can teach us a lot.

We can be very proud of ourselves, but this adventure ain't over yet. And this last case is going to really push us to our spooky limits.

Because it's been fun being cartoon characters, having special powers like travelling through time and getting to appear and disappear whenever we want, but it's time to get **real** again, and there is a world of difference between peeking in curiously on other people's hauntings and actually experiencing one yourself.

Which is perhaps why my teeth are chattering as I fumble in the rainy darkness, trying to put up my tent. I look over at Phil. He's an experienced climber; his tent's already up and he's now trying to light a fire under the one bit of shelter this ruined house still offers.

Phil is the reason I'm here, shivering, ten miles from the warmth and comfort of the nearest town, wishing I'd worn my thermal underwear. He is a very ordinary-looking man, bald with twinkly eyes and a big smile. He works as a locksmith, rescuing people who've locked themselves out of their houses or forgotten the combination to their jewellery safe. He is most definitely not the sort of person you'd expect to tell you a ghost story, but, more than 50 years ago, when he was still a teenager, he believes he witnessed a haunting right here in this very house, and now he wants me to experience it with him. And you can join us too.

Before I first met Phil a few years ago, if you'd asked me to tick a box, I'd have been pretty much **#TeamSceptic** all the way. I'd always loved ghost stories. I secretly wished ghosts were real, but in my heart, I didn't believe.

But then I heard Phil's story, and there was something about how he described what had happened to him that sent a ginormous shiver down my spine and made me think, *OK, maybe this could all be real.*

People have told ghost stories around campfires ever since prehistoric times, so now, by the flickering flames of our fire, let me tell you Phil's story.

It starts in **February 1974**. He and his friend Jimmy are out hiking, close to the town of Kinlochleven, here in the Scottish Highlands. This is a stunning part of the world, where you are likely to see stags with giant antlers roaming the hills and majestic golden eagles flying casually over your head.

Phil and Jimmy are part of a local climbing club, but even for experienced climbers like them, the weather in February that year is a challenge. Snow lies thick on the ground and the air is bitterly cold. They know they'll have to find somewhere indoors to sleep tonight, but the great thing about this part of Scotland is that there are loads of bothies. A 'bothy' is a little hut or cottage that is always open for climbers and hikers. Whatever the time of day or night, you can arrive and find a place to sleep and keep warm. And Phil has heard of one these bothies not too far from where they are walking. It's called **Luibeilt**.

It's still daylight when Phil and Jimmy arrive there. It turns out that Luibeilt is a two-storey cottage by a river – it looks nicer than the average stone hut they often find themselves staying in and, when they go inside, they discover it even has furniture, as if somebody has actually been living there. There's a bookcase with books on, and upstairs they find an old metal bed that's been taken apart and left in pieces, and strangely, a big stone boulder on a window ledge.

Pronounced loo-ee-belt. *It's a* **Gaelic** *name. Gaelic is the native language of Scotland, which has existed since before the Scots learned English.*

Oddest of all, though, they find a table downstairs that has been laid for Christmas dinner. Given that it's now well over a month since Christmas, this seems very strange indeed. The whole house has the feel of somewhere that's been abandoned – as if whoever lived here ran off in the middle of their Christmas meal and have not been back since.

Phil can't help but think of stories he heard as a kid about the *Mary Celeste* – a 'ghost ship' that was found adrift in the 1800s with everything on board completely as normal, a full larder of food and provisions, but no sign of the crew – it was if they had simply disappeared without a trace.

It happened in December 1872. The crew were never found and no one knows what happened to them. It is one of history's great unsolved mysteries.

But it is very cold and snowy outside, so even if it does seem a bit odd, Phil and Jimmy are not going to pass up this opportunity to have a nice dry place to stay for the night. As it gets dark, they chat and cook themselves some food on their camping stove then eat by candlelight, and, around midnight, they climb into their sleeping bags and blow their candles out.

It is totally pitch-black. The kind of darkness you can't find in a city – solid, heavy and total.

And then, just a moment later, is when the **noise** starts.

It comes from directly above them. At first, it's footsteps. We've encountered those before on our adventures at Stacey's school, so I wouldn't expect an experienced paranormal investigator like you to get too worried about that, but these ones are different. They seemingly walk round and round in circles and then, alongside the footsteps, there is the sound of the bits of metal bed frame being dragged around, and the stone boulder on the window ledge rolling across the floor!

---

*I guess you'd call that **rock 'n' roll**?*

Phil and Jimmy are confused. They'd checked the house and there was no one else there. Maybe another climber snuck in? But why would they be rearranging the bed or rolling a big stone about 🗿 this late at night? And why walk round and round and round? Still, they decide that's what it must be. They're tired, it's cold and dark, they don't really feel like going upstairs to investigate, and so they eventually drift off to sleep.

But not for long. At 1 a.m. the living room where they are sleeping suddenly erupts like a volcano! Things are flying around – **a blizzard of objects!** Books shoot off the bookcase towards them, climbing gear swirls about, and, if you thought LEGO bricks were dangerous, then how about this – Phil's ice axe, which he carries with him for going up icy mountains, flies through the air, just past his nose!

It is full-on poltergeist activity of the most dangerous kind! Phil is terrified and stunned, but mostly terrified, not wanting to

---

🗿 *Maybe he was a fan of the* **Rolling Stones?** *Ask your parents who they are if you don't get this joke!*

believe his eyes as objects shoot towards him through the darkness like X-wings attacking the Death Star trench in *Star Wars*. Somehow he manages to light a candle, just long enough to illuminate a cascade of books throwing themselves off the shelves like lemmings, but then the candle goes flying too, as if someone has just kicked it away! And now he's **really panicking**, his heart beating so loudly Jimmy can actually hear it!

And then, as things finally come to rest, the footsteps start again above. Only this time they aren't walking in circles; they walk out of the bedroom and then come down the stairs, treading slowly towards where Phil and Jimmy are, quivering in their sleeping bags!

CLUNK CLUNK CLUNK CLUNK

Phil springs up, instinctively grabbing his ice axe for protection, and waits by the door to the stairs, no longer at all sure that whoever's in this house is just another climber come to sleep the night. In fact, he feels like he and Jimmy might really be in danger here as the footsteps reach the bottom of the stairs . . .

CLUNK CLUNK **CLUNK** . . .

And then . . . they stop!

CLUNK

It's like someone is waiting on the other side of the door. **Gulp**. Phil's heart is beating faster than an express train as he throws open the door and —

There's no one there.

How could somebody make that much noise coming down the stairs, but then disappear without a trace?

This is enough for Phil and Jimmy. As quick as they can, they pack up their stuff and get out of that house, walking through the cold dark night all the way back to Kinlochleven.

And that, you would imagine, is the last time Phil ever goes anywhere near that house called Luibeilt.

Well, you would imagine wrong.

Because that night shocked and confused Phil so much, he could never forget it. He wanted to understand how it was possible that objects could fly through the air or footsteps could walk down stairs when no one was there. So he decided he needed to go back, to confront the house and try to find answers. He returned to Luibeilt, this time taking a different friend with him. And, on that second night, they again heard strange noises, and Phil still didn't understand. So he went back for a third trip and, that time, he found graffiti painted on the wall of Luibeilt saying, '*Do not sleep in this house. This house is haunted.*' Which means that he and his friends weren't the **only** people to have experienced things there! Other people had slept in the house and got spooked out and left this warning!

This made Phil feel relieved in one way, because it meant he hadn't been imagining it, but it also freaked him out because it meant something real was actually happening in this strange, lonely house.

It troubled him his whole life. Many years later, when he was no longer a young man, he started posting on the internet, trying to find some of the other people who'd also stayed at Luibeilt. And he did, and they told him about how they too had heard footsteps and witnessed strange things. All of which means we now have a very big question to answer . . .

What is going on at Luibeilt and is it the most haunted house in Britain? 🐚

In total, Phil has now visited the house seven times, as he struggles to solve this mystery. And when he wrote to me to ask for help, I became drawn into the mystery too, which is why I have now travelled with him to Luibeilt tonight.

Because that's where we are, in case you were wondering. Here in the house where it all happened. Over the years, the building has fallen apart; it's very different now to the place Phil and Jimmy stayed in in 1974. There are no upstairs rooms any more, all the floors have fallen in and most of the walls have fallen down. But I can still feel a **strange atmosphere** as I sit here by the light of our campfire. So, as we toast some marshmallows

---

🐚 *OK, I admit it, that is **two** big questions.*

for dinner, it feels like a good time for us to start discussing some theories. Let me scribble them down on this soggy bit of paper!

#TeamBeliever
theory –
Who do you think you are
haunted by?

There's a programme on TV called *Who Do You Think You Are?* where celebrities trace their family trees to find out who they are descended from. They almost always find strange mysteries in their family's past and sometimes sad things that have happened to their ancestors. And investigating a haunting can be a bit like that – except you're tracing the family tree of a house.

Because if you are #TeamBeliever, then one of the first questions has to be: could the ghost be

....

It's very important to eat healthily. But not when you are on a ghost hunt!

someone who used to live in the house and has returned to haunt it?

To answer that, we need to try and find someone who once lived in the house, who might have a reason to return from the dead or who could be connected to the ghostly activity we are witnessing. An easy example of this would be if we heard a disembodied voice saying, '**My name is Bob!**', we could check the records and find out if a man called Bob lived in that house a hundred years ago. If he did, the chances are he's your ghost.

So basically, we have to trace the house's family tree, looking at all the people who ever lived – and maybe died – there!

There are lots of different ways to do this. We could read through the electoral registers, which are official documents that show a list of who is registered to vote in elections. These only show people living at each house who are over 18 though, as nobody under that age can vote. You can also

---

*If only **all** hauntings were as easy to solve as that!*

A silly rule, I know. I reckon if kids could vote, the world would be a better place.

check census records. A **census** is a big survey the government does every ten years where they collect a record of everyone living in the country and details about them such as age, what job they do and if they are married. Checking the census records will show you everyone who lived in a house.

FIND THE FAMILY TREE OF YOUR HOUSE!

Electoral registers and census records are normally available online, or you can often go to look at the original documents wherever they are kept in your area – it's normally a library or a town hall. So why don't you ask your parents for help to check out the history of the building you live in?

How old is your house or apartment? How many families lived there before yours? Maybe you will find interesting people that did cool jobs who lived there in the past. If you live in a modern building, you could try to find out what stood on the land before your house was built. Just think about everyone who ever lived there and all the stories they could tell!

One other thing that I always do when I am investigating a haunting is I check **newspaper archives**. There are a few of them online, like the *British Newspaper Archive*. You usually have to pay for a subscription, but they are very useful for finding out stories about things that happened at a certain address – for instance, if there have been any dramatic deaths there that might have been reported in a local newspaper.

Phil and I have done a **LOT** of research on Luibeilt and we were able to find out some very interesting things. Things that will blow your mind.

Luibeilt had been a family house right up to just before Phil and Jimmy turned up there in 1974. Can you imagine how **tough** life would have been living there, so far away from anywhere else, without electricity or running water? Not many people could cope with that. And the family living there had indeed left the house at Christmas, just after the birth of their baby, on the orders of a local doctor who told them it wasn't a safe place to bring up a child. So this explains the mystery of that uneaten Christmas dinner – they were forced to leave before they could eat it!

But wading back through the newspaper archive, we were able to find out even more about the people who'd lived at Luibeilt over the centuries. That is when we came across it – a newspaper report that might just hold a major clue! When we read it, the hairs stood up on our heads. Well, on my head. Phil is bald. But I'm pretty sure his scalp tingled. Because this newspaper report led us to make another very spooky discovery.

The article was a sad story in a local newspaper about a man called **John McAlpine** who had lived in the house and worked in the area, controlling the population of deer. One day in **1890,** his wife found him dead in the outhouse, a small building next to the main house where the family stored their provisions. The newspaper article jumped out at us for two reasons – one was that John McAlpine had actually died *at* Luibeilt, which seems like a potential reason to be stuck there as a ghost. The second reason was even more intriguing. And if my hair was already standing on end, this is when it almost shot out of its roots. Because, at the time that Phil and Jimmy went to stay in Luibeilt, Phil was living in Glasgow, the largest city in Scotland, in a house on a road called Gibson Street. And, as we were tracking down the history of John McAlpine, trying to discover everything we could about him, we found out something incredible. It seemed that John, as a child, had actually lived in the **very same house** on Gibson Street, about 120 years before Phil!!!

Is this just a coincidence? Or was there some kind of connection across all those years that drew Phil and John together, so that Phil was haunted by John's ghost? What do you think? I feel a tingle down my spine just thinking about it. It's this kind of detective work that is one of my **favourite** bits of investigating a haunting!

But let's not get too carried away. It's important to consider the sceptic possibilities too. And, as this is our final case, I have not just one **#TEAMSCEPTIC** theory for you, but two!

One thing we should definitely mention is just how cold it was that night in February 1974. I explained earlier how the dark can make us imagine things, and the cold can really affect our

---

Well, that and eating biscuits!

Look back at pages 53–56!

judgement too. It is actually possible to get so cold that you develop a condition called hypothermia, which is when your body starts to shut down because it cannot cope at such a low temperature. This can lead to hallucinations. It's the sort of thing that happens to polar explorers.

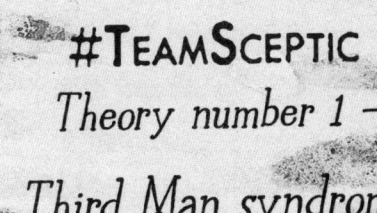

#TeamSceptic
Theory number 1 –
Third Man syndrome

Ernest Shackleton was an explorer who led an expedition to the Antarctic from 1914 to 1917 (it was a long expedition!). He wrote a book about it and described how he and his team had often felt they had an extra person with them. It seems that the cold was making them hallucinate a bonus team member, perhaps to give them hope and comfort.

The famous poet T. S. Eliot  wrote a poem about Shackleton, which contained the line, 'Who is the third who walks always beside you?'. This gave us the term 'Third Man Syndrome', which psychologists now use to describe what happened to Shackleton's team. Experts believe it can affect people in extreme situations – such as intense cold or where there is a lack of oxygen – people such as climbers and pilots. It's a sensation that you are not alone, that another person is there with you.

Some psychologists think this could also help explain hauntings, either because the person who feels haunted is too cold, or because the fear they are experiencing acts in the same way as the cold – pushing that person into an extreme mental and physical state.

But we'd have to be talking about some pretty extreme freezing cold to make Phil and Jimmy hallucinate, and I'm not sure they ever got **that** chilly –

⌣ *He wrote the poems that the musical* Cats *is based on.*

they were able to escape, after all, and walk back to safety. So how else could we explain books flying off a shelf, objects flying across a room and strange noises overhead?

#TeamSceptic
Theory number 2 –
Could it have been an earthquake?

I know what you're going to say: **earthquakes** don't happen in the UK! But actually they do, and they happen more often than you might think. In fact, if you google where you live, you might find there has been an earthquake there. The reason we don't know much about them is that they are usually very minor tremors, nothing like the quakes that affect other parts of the world and cause damage to towns and cities. But every so often there is an earthquake that is strong enough to shake buildings and cause some damage. In 2007 there was an earthquake in Kent, in southern England, which was so strong it damaged 474 houses!

The way earthquakes work is that the Earth's crust is made up of large sections called **tectonic plates**. These plates are moving constantly, but very **very** slowly, either towards or away from each other. The places where the plates meet are called **fault-lines** – basically cracks or breaks in the Earth's crust. When the plates try to move past each other but get stuck, pressure can build up along these fault-lines. Sometimes that pressure becomes too much and all the stored energy is released, causing an earthquake! And – guess what – there are several fault-lines that run through Scotland! Is it possible that what Phil and Jimmy experienced was actually a minor earthquake, that was strong enough to make books fall off a shelf and a candle fall over?

How are you feeling about the Luibeilt haunting?

 **#TeamBeliever**

#TeamSceptic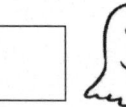

It's a lot to think about, and it's definitely time for bed, so you and Ellen had better go off to your own tents[◌] while I try to get some sleep. I'm sharing a tent with my friend **Simon** who I make my podcast with. He's come with us to record everything that happens. He falls asleep before I do. My thoughts are still racing, trying to make sense of Phil's experiences, but eventually I do doze off...

Until...

At a certain time in the night, I wake, and I can hear...

Footsteps.

Only it doesn't sound like they are on the grass surrounding my tent. It sounds like they're on **floorboards**.

Floorboards that don't exist any more.

Blimey. Holy moly. OMG. Am I really experiencing the same sounds Phil heard all those years ago? Or am I *imagining them* because he told me about it? Is this cognitive bias in action – me hearing random noises and assuming they are footsteps?

But what else sounds like footsteps?

You did bring one, didn't you? Otherwise you might have to find a way to camp under your bedsheet!

I am eventually able to get back to sleep. The next morning, when I wake up, I ask my friend Simon how he slept.

He tells me he woke in the night too.

'I didn't hear any footsteps,' he says.

I am slightly disappointed.

'But I did hear a woman scream.'

WHAT???
ARE YOU **SERIOUS????**

Simon believes he heard a woman **screaming**, here where we are camping – which is right next to the outhouse where John McAlpine's wife found him dead one day! A shiver runs right through me at the thought. Have we just experienced our very own haunting?

My knees are **definitely** trembling now. I'll meet you in the next chapter, shall I? And find those biscuits, because I am very definitely going to need a chocolate digestive.

CHAPTER 13

THE THIRD TEAM

In which we try to make sense of
everything we have seen and heard,
which is not going to be easy.

Munch munch munch.

Excuse me, but after the cold, the rain and the shiver-inducing night-time sounds, I really needed that biscuit.

So this it, I guess. Our last chapter together. Whose idea was it to do **13 chapters?** Don't they know the number 13 is supposed to bring bad luck?[☾] Or perhaps you think that's just a silly old superstition? Something human beings have invented to spook ourselves.

And is that what ghosts are? A human invention, a creepy tale to make our tummies tingle and our hair stand on end?[☾]

Or are they really the dead come back to life? Either literally, walking around again in the places they used to live, or perhaps somehow being replayed like supernatural video recordings?

At the beginning of this book, I asked you to write down on a bit of paper whether you felt

----

☾ *Did you know that a fear of the number 13 is called* triskaidekaphobia. *Try saying* **that** *with a mouthful of biscuit!*

☾ *Unless you are* **Phil**. *Sorry, Phil!*

you were **#TeamBeliever** or **#TeamSceptic**. I'm hoping that you have been using that bit of paper as a bookmark like I suggested, and can now unfold it and look at what you wrote.

Is that still how you feel? Or have you changed your mind as we have been on this journey together?

Have you become more of a believer or more of a sceptic?

Or do we perhaps need to introduce a third team?

#TeamNotSure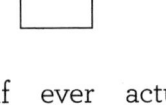

Because unless you yourself ever actually experience a haunting, you're probably never going to be completely certain one way or another, and I think it's OK to accept that.

We live in a world where people are always demanding that you **take sides**. If you support one football team, you're told that you shouldn't like the fans of another team. If you vote for one political party, you are told to disagree with people who vote for the others. All across the globe, people are arguing, clashing with each other – like those tectonic plates!

Our world can feel quite divided, all because one group of people feels really strongly about one thing and another group feels really strongly about something else.

But sometimes it is OK to be in the middle, to sit there and listen to **both** sides. To enjoy hearing someone's strange spooky story and then say to yourself, 'You know what, I'm not completely sure what I think happened, but I'm going to have fun trying to find out.'

It's OK to keep an open mind.

Because this is a journey that we have only just begun. There are so many questions left for us to answer, so many more adventures to be had. As I finish writing these final words of the book, I can already hear my inbox pinging with new emails from people who feel they have been haunted, new cases to investigate.

So I'm hoping you're not too busy, because I'm going to need your help again. You can keep that bedsheet for now and I'll see you very soon for some more paranormal adventures.

....

Maybe ask your parents to wash the **egg** *and* **chocolate stains** *off.*

Until then, sleep well, don't have nightmares, and remember your bedroom is the same place in the dark as it is in the day, and that the dressing gown hanging on your door is just a dressing gown, nothing ghostly. (Unless, of course, it is a **haunted** dressing gown, in which case that sounds completely and utterly cool – can I come and investigate it?)

Bye for now. Stay spooky.

Danny

X63 243
76 68
26 N1

I hope you've enjoyed reading this book as much as I've enjoyed writing it. If you want to know more about what I do, you can visit my website: **www.dannyrobins.com**, where you can find out about my podcasts, TV programmes, books, tours and live shows. Sometimes I visit schools, so why not tell your teacher to invite me to yours? (Just make sure they have some biscuits!)

I love hearing from people who are as interested in ghosts as I am, so if you want to email me, you can write to **danny@dannyrobins.com** (make sure you get permission from a parent or guardian first!). Why don't you let me know what you thought of the book, tell me a ghost story if you've got one, hit me with some of your own **#TeamBeliever** or **#TeamSceptic** theories on the cases, or just tell me your favourite ghost joke. Ellen would also love to see your **drawings** of some of your favourite scenes from the book.

Speak soon!

....

So would I! Maybe you can draw your own cartoon version of me. If so, can you make my nose a bit smaller?

Writing a book involves more people than you might think! I have a lot of lovely friends, family and colleagues who have supported me in different ways as I've been writing *Do You Believe in Ghosts?*, and I'd like to give them all a big shout-out here!

First off, a

massive thanks

to all of the witnesses I spoke to –
Graham for Enfield,
Matt for Hangar K17,
Stacey for the Haunted Toilet
and Phil for Luibeilt.

I think it takes bravery to tell everyone you might have seen a ghost, and I am very grateful that you trusted me with your stories.

....

Normally when authors write thank yous, it's a bit boring, but I think you should read these because there is a **SPECIAL SURPRISE** *at the end!*

An **ENORMOUS** THANK YOU

(and yes, I really am *shouting* that) to Ellen for her fantastic, funny illustrations. I'm so glad we met! I'd also like to thank my editor at Puffin Books, the brilliant Fenella Bates – none of this would have happened without you; thank you for believing in me and the book! Also our excellent designer, Andrea Kearney, for making mine and Ellen's work look so blooming great and being such a fun collaborator. And Sarah Malley, our text designer, who was full of brilliant ideas of how to make the book as fun to read as possible, including doing crazy stuff like **THIS!**

Thanks to Sarah Connelly, who copy-edited the book – that's the bit of the process where someone makes sure everything I have said is factually correct and checks my grammar and spelling. It's a bit like having a really nice teacher check your work, and Sarah has been great, never once missing a spelling mistoke.

Thanks to my super-duper literary agent, Cathryn Summerhayes – I'm so glad we met too, and I am grateful for all your wisdom and support. Thanks also to my wonderful presenting agent, Jacquie Drewe, who is a huge part of all of this and also super wise!

A big shout-out to everyone at the BBC who is involved with my *Uncanny* podcasts and TV series, especially Rhian Roberts, Paula McDonnell, Mohit Bakaya, Jack Bootle and Alan Holland, and to everyone who works with me on the *Uncanny Live* tour – Sam, Pam, Rhys, Jack and Katy. If you come to see us on tour you might meet them, 👻 and I'll sign this book for you!

Thanks to the dream team at my production company, Uncanny Media – Rachael, Tam, Kerry, Liz, Linz and, most of all, Nancy who, as ever, has been a great help with research and fielding all of the emails that come in to me full of exciting new ghost stories to investigate!

A **ginormous** thanks

to my good friend Simon Barnard, who makes the *Uncanny* podcast with me, and came on that spook-tastic trip to Luibeilt, getting rather wet and a little freaked out in the process. And thanks to Ciaran O'Keeffe, Evelyn Hollow, Deborah Hyde, Chris French, and all the other *Uncanny* experts from both #TeamBeliever and #TeamSceptic who have helped me learn more about the paranormal. I love the fact that, whatever we believe or don't believe, we all get on so well and enjoy these intriguing stories together.

👻 *They are quite nice and occasionally have* **biscuits** *they might share.*

And last

but very definitely not least, a

HUUUUGGGE

thank you to my wife, Eva,
and my children, Leo and Max. I love you all more
than words can say. Thanks for putting up with me writing this
book when sometimes I should have been hanging out having
fun with you – and Leo and Max, I hope you like the
cool cartoon versions of you Ellen has drawn!

Did I say last? *There is one more thank you actually.*
It's a really super important one that I couldn't
possibly forget. Someone who has been so important
throughout this whole book, someone who
I now consider a friend. But you'll have to
turn the page to find out who it is.

It's . . .

YOU.